From Athens to America

Readings in Western Philosophy

Paul Dykes & John C. Powell

Stillwater, Oklahoma
U.S.A.

NEW FORUMS PRESS INC.

Published in the United States of America
by New Forums Press, Inc. 1018 S. Lewis St.
Stillwater, OK 74074
www.newforums.com

Copyright © 2002 by New Forums Press, Inc.

All rights reserved. No part of this publication may be reproduced or transmitted in any form or by any means, electronic or mechanical, including photocopy, or any information storage or retrieval system, without permission in writing from the publisher.

Library of Congress Cataloging-in-Publication Data Pending

This book may be ordered in bulk quantities at discount from New Forums Press, Inc., P.O. Box 876, Stillwater, OK 74076 [Federal I.D. No. 73 1123239]. Printed in the United States of America.

ISBN 10: 1-58107-058-6
ISBN 13: 978-1-581070-58-3

Introduction

These readings from the literature of western philosophy have been collected to serve a practical classroom purpose: to make available to students a sampling of the ideas of some of history's great thinkers on the subject of human values. The selection is eclectic but not random. The excerpts included have been used in philosophy classes and have been the basis for thoughtful and spirited student discussions.

The intent of the anthologists is not to instill values but to encourage readers to test their own assumptions and opinions against a variety of ideas and to emerge from the encounter better prepared to shape the values by which they will live their own lives.

We thank Heritage Hall School of Oklahoma City for providing the support that made this publication possible. The readings reflect no more—nor less—than the convictions of those who wrote them. We encourage attention to the selections; agreement or disagreement is the option of the reader.

Dr. John C. Powell
Dean of Faculty
Heritage Hall School
Oklahoma City, Oklahoma

Paul Dykes
English Faculty
Booker T. Washington H.S.
Tulsa, Oklahoma

Contents

Introduction iii

PLATO 1
   From The Apology of Socrates 2
   From The Republic (Book One) 8
   From The Republic (Book Two) 16
   From The Republic (Book Four) 28
   From The Republic (Book Seven) 42

ARISTOTLE 46
   From The Nichomachean Ethics (Book One) 47
   From The Nichomachean Ethics (Book Two) 56

EPICURUS 65
   From his letter to Menoecius 66

EPICTETUS 69
   From The Enchiridion 70

MARCUS AURELIUS 83
   From Meditations 84

AUGUSTINE 94
   From The Confessions 95

FRANCIS BACON 104
   From Novum Organum 105

THOMAS HOBBES 108
   From Leviathan 110

RENE DESCARTES 119
   From Discourse on Method 120

BENEDICT SPINOZA 129
    From On the Improvement of the Understanding 130

JOHN LOCKE 135
    From Essay Concerning Human Understanding 136

JEAN JACQUES ROUSSEAU 143
    From The Social Contract 145

DAVID HUME 151
    From Essays, Moral and Political 152

IMMANUEL KANT 161
    From The Fundamental Principles of the Metaphysics of Morals 162

G.W.F. HEGEL 169
    From The Philosophy of Religion 170

ARTHUR SCHOPENHAUER 179
    From On the Basis of Morality 180

SOREN KIERKEGAARD 188
    From The Attack on Christendom 189

JOHN STUART MILL 195
    From Utilitarianism 196

FRIEDRICH NIETZSCHE 205
    From Beyond Good and Evil 207

WILLIAM JAMES 213
    From The Will to Believe 214

Sources 223

PLATO

(428-348)

"The difficulty, my friends, is not to avoid death, but to avoid unrighteousness; for that runs faster than death."

In the dialogue of Plato the reader encounters Socrates who, although not the first Greek to raise questions about behavior, virtue, and human purpose, stands as the embodiment of ethical inquiry. The life of Socrates (c. 469 – 399) spans the golden age of Athenian achievement, and Plato consistently casts Socrates as the narrator in his dialogues. In so doing the younger Plato (428 – 348) forever linked his name with that of his revered teacher. And despite their differences in age and background Socrates, the impoverished son of an artisan/laborer, and Plato, descended on both sides of his family from Athenian aristocracy, stand together at the beginning of moral philosophy in western civilization.

The excerpts that follow are written by Plato; there is no record of any written work by Socrates. *The Apology* is not a verbatim account of what Socrates said to the jury on the day he was tried, found guilty, and was sentenced to death. It is, instead, an impression written after the event by his devoted younger friend and represents the essence of the older man's temperament and intellect.

Selections from *The Republic*, one of the masterpieces of world literature, dramatize further the legacy of Socrates as the examiner of life and suggest in some measure the style of Plato's writing and the substance of his ideas.

THE APOLOGY

PLATO

(At this point in his trial Socrates has been found guilty by the jurors and must counter with his own argument the demand of his accusers that he be put to death.)

There are many reasons why I am not grieved, O men of Athens, at the vote of condemnation. I expected it, and am only surprised that the votes are so nearly equal; for I had thought that the majority against me would have been far larger; but now, had thirty votes gone over to the other side, I should have been acquitted. And I may say, I think, that I have escaped Meletus. I may say more; for without the assistance of Anytus and Lycon, any one may see that he would not have had a fifth part of the votes, as the law requires, in which case he would have incurred a fine of a thousand drachmae.

And so he proposes death as the penalty. And what shall I propose on my part, O men of Athens? Clearly that which is my due. And what is my due? What return shall be made to the man who has never had the wit to be idle during his whole life; but has been careless of what the many care for—wealth, and family interests, and military offices, and speaking in the assembly, and magistracies, and plots, and parties. Reflecting that I was really too honest a man to be a politician and live, I did not go where I could do no good to you or to myself; but where I could do the greatest good privately to every one of you, thither I went, and sought to persuade every man among you that he must look to himself, and seek virtue and wisdom before he looks to his private interests, and look to the state before he looks to the interests of the state; and that this should be the order which he observes in all his actions. What shall be done to such an one? Doubtless some good thing, O men of Athens, if he has his reward; and the good should be of a kind suitable to him. What would be a reward suitable to a poor man who is your benefactor, and who desires leisure that he may instruct you? There can be no reward so fitting as maintenance in the Prytaneum, O men of Athens, a reward which he deserves far more than the citizen who has won the prize at Olympia in the horse or chariot race, whether the chariots were drawn by two horses or by many. For I am in want, and he has enough; and he only gives you the appearance of happiness, and I give you the reality. And if I am to estimate the penalty fairly, I should say that maintenance in the Prytaneum is the just return.

Perhaps you think that I am braving you in what I am saying now, as in what I said before about the tears and prayers. But this is not so. I speak rather because I am convinced that I never intentionally wronged any one, although I cannot convince you—the time has been too short; if there were a law at Athens, as there is in other cities, that a capital cause should not be decided in one day, then I believe that I should have convinced you. But I cannot in a moment refute great slanders; and, as I am convinced that I never wronged another, I will assuredly not wrong myself. I will not say of myself that I deserve evil, or propose any penalty. Why should I? Because I am afraid of the penalty of death which Meletus proposes? When I do not know whether death is a good or an evil, why should I propose a penalty which would certainly be an evil? Shall I say imprisonment? And why should I live in prison, and be the slave of the magistrates of the year—of the Eleven? Or shall the penalty be a fine, and imprisonment until the fine is paid? There is the same objection. I should have to lie in prison, for money I have none, and cannot pay. And if I say exile (and this may possibly be the penalty which you will affix), I must indeed be blinded by the love of life, if I am so irrational as to expect that when you, who are my own citizens, cannot endure my discourses and words, and have found them so grievous and odious that you will have no more of them, others are likely to endure me. No indeed, men of Athens, that is not very likely. And what a life should I lead, at my age, wandering from city to city, ever changing my place of exile, and always being driven out! For I am quite sure that wherever I go, there, as here, the young men will flock to me; and if I drive them away, their elders will drive me out at their request; and if I let them come, their fathers and friends will drive me out for their sakes.

Some one will say: Yes, Socrates, but cannot you hold your tongue, and then you may go into a foreign city, and no one will interfere with you? Now I have great difficulty in making you understand my answer to this. For if I tell you that to do as you say would be a disobedience to the God, and therefore that I cannot hold my tongue, you will not believe that I am serious; and if I say again that daily to discourse about virtue, and of those other things about which you hear me examining myself and others, is the greatest good of man, and that the unexamined life is not worth living, you are still less likely to believe me. Yet I say what is true, although a thing of which it is hard for me to persuade you. Also, I have never been accustomed to think that I deserve to suffer any harm. Had I money I might have estimated the offence at what I was able to pay, and not have been much the worse. But I have none, and therefore I must ask you to proportion the fine to my means. Well, perhaps I could afford a mina, and therefore I propose that penalty: Plato, Crito, Critobulus, and Apollodorus, my friends here, bid me say thirty minae, and they will be the sureties. Let thirty minae be the penalty; for which sum they will be ample security to you.

(The decision of the jurors, by a greater margin than by which they found Socrates guilty, is that he suffer capital punishment. What follows is his response, both to those who voted for his death and to those who stood by him.)

Not much time will be gained, O Athenians, in return for the evil name which you will get from the detractors of the city, who will say that you killed Socrates, a wise man; for they will call me wise, even though I am not wise, when they want to reproach you. If you had waited a little while, your desire would have been fulfilled in the course of nature. For I am far advanced in years, as you may perceive, and not far from death. I am speaking now not to all of you, but only to those who have condemned me to death. And I have another thing to say to them: You think that I was convicted because I have no words of the sort which would have procured my acquittal—I mean, if I had thought fit to leave nothing undone or unsaid. Not so; the deficiency which led to my conviction was not of words—certainly not. But I had not the boldness or impudence or inclination to address you as you would have liked me to do, weeping and wailing and lamenting, and saying and doing many things which you have been accustomed to hear from others, and which, as I maintain, are unworthy of me. I thought at the time that I ought not to do anything common or mean when in danger: nor do I now repent of the style of my defence; I would rather die having spoken after my manner, than speak in your manner and live. For neither in war not yet at law ought I or any man to use every way of escaping death. Often in battle there can be no doubt that if a man will throw away his arms, and fall on his knees before his pursuers, he may escape death; and in other dangers there are other ways of escaping death, if a man is willing to say and do anything. The difficulty, my friends, is not to avoid death, but to avoid unrighteousness; for that runs faster than death. I am old and move slowly, and the slower runner has overtaken me, and my accusers are keen and quick, and the faster runner, who is unrighteousness, has overtaken them. And now I depart hence condemned by you to suffer the penalty of death,—they too go their ways condemned by the truth to suffer the penalty of villainy and wrong; and I must abide by my award—let them abide by theirs. I suppose that these things may be regarded as fated,—and I think that they are well.

And now, O men who have condemned me, I would fain prophesy to you; for I am about to die, and in the hour of death men are gifted with prophetic power. And I prophesy to you who are my murderers, that immediately after my departure punishment far heavier than you have inflicted on me will surely await you. Me you have killed because you wanted to escape the accuser, and not to give an account of your lives. But that will not be as you suppose: far otherwise. For I say that there will be more accusers of you than there are now; accusers whom hitherto I have restrained: and as they are younger they will be more inconsiderate with you, and you will be more offended at them. If you think that by killing men you can prevent some one from censuring your evil lives, you are mistaken; that is not a way of escape which is either possible or honourable; the easiest and the noblest way is not to be disabling others, but to be improving yourselves. This is the prophecy which I utter before my departure to the judges who have condemned me.

Friends, who would have acquitted me, I would like also to talk with you about the thing which has come to pass, while the magistrates are busy, and before I go to the place at which I must die. Stay then a little, for we may as well talk with one another while there is time. You are my friends, and I should like to show you the meaning of this event which has happened to me. O my judges—for you I may truly call judges—I should like to tell you of a wonderful circumstance. Hitherto the divine faculty of which the internal oracle is the source has constantly been in the habit of opposing me even about trifles, if I was going to make a slip or error in any matter; and now as you see there has come upon me that which may be thought, and is generally believed to be, the last and worst evil. But the oracle made no sign of opposition, either when I was leaving my house in the morning, or when I was on my way to the court, or while I was speaking, at anything which I was going to say; and yet I have often been stopped in the middle of a speech, but now in nothing I either said or did touching the matter in hand has the oracle opposed me. What do I take to be the explanation of this silence? I will tell you. It is an intimation that what has happened to me is a good, and that those of us who think that death is an evil are in error. For the customary sign would surely have opposed me had I been going to evil and not to good.

Let us reflect in another way, and we shall see that there is a great reason to hope that death is a good; for one of two things—either death is a state of nothingness and utter unconsciousness, or, as men say, there is a change and migration of the soul from this world to another. Now if you suppose that there is no consciousness, but a sleep like the sleep of him who is undisturbed even by dreams, death will be an unspeakable gain. For if a person were to select the night in which his sleep was undisturbed even by dreams, and were to compare with this the other days and nights of his life, and then were to tell us how many days and nights he had passed in the course of his life better and more pleasantly than this one, I think that any man, I will not say a private man, but even the great king will not find many such days or nights, when compared with the others. Now if death be of such a nature, I say that to die is gain; for eternity is then only a single night. But if death is the journey to another place, and there, as men say, all the dead abide, what good, O my friends and judges, can be greater than this? If indeed when the pilgrim arrives in the world below, he is delivered from the professors of justice in this world, and finds the true judges who are said to give judgment there, Minos and Rhadamanthus and Aeacus and Triptolemus, and other sons of God who were righteous in their own life, that pilgrimage will be worth making. What would not a man give if he might converse with Orpheus and Musaeus and Hesiod and Homer? Nay, if this be true, let me die again and again. I myself, too, shall have a wonderful interest in there meeting and conversing with Palamedes, and Ajax the son of Telamon, and any other ancient hero who has suffered death through an unjust judgment; and there will be no small pleasure, as I think, in comparing my own sufferings with theirs. Above all, I shall then be able to continue my search into true and false knowledge; as in this world, so also in the next; and I shall find out who is wise, and who pretends to be wise, and is not. What would not a man give, O judges, to be able to examine the leader of the great Trojan expedition; or Odysseus or Sisyphus, or numberless others, men and women too! What infinite delight would there be in conversing with them and asking them questions! In another world they do not put a man to death for asking questions: assuredly not. For besides being happier than we are, they will be immortal, if what is said is true.

Wherefore, O judges, be of good cheer about death, and know of a certainty, that no evil can happen to a good man, either in life or after death. He and his are not neglected by the gods; nor has my own approaching end happened by mere chance. But I see clearly that the time had arrived when it was better for me to die and be released from trouble; wherefore the oracle gave no sign. For which reason, also, I am not angry with my condemners, or with my accusers; they have done me no harm, although they did not mean to do me any good; and for this I may gently blame them.

Still I have a favour to ask of them. When my sons are grown up, I would ask you, O my friends, to punish them; and I would have you trouble them, as I have troubled you, if they seem to care about riches, or anything, more than about virtue; or if they pretend to be something when they are really nothing,—then reprove them, as I have reproved you, for not caring about that for which they ought to care, and thinking that they are something when they are really nothing. And if you do this, both I and my sons will have received justice at your hands.

The hour of departure has arrived, and we go our ways—I to die, and you to live. Which is better God only knows.

THE REPUBLIC

PLATO

Book I

(The Republic begins as an inquiry into the nature of justice. In book one Socrates questions the definition of justice offered by Thrasymachus, one of the Sophists of Athens.)

Several times in the course of the discussion Thrasymachus had made an attempt to get the argument into his own hands, and had been put down by the rest of the company, who wanted to hear the end. But when Polemarchus and I had done speaking and there was a pause, he could no longer hold his peace; and, gathering himself up, he came at us like a wild beast, seeking to devour us. We were quite panic-stricken at the sight of him.

He roared out to the whole company: What folly, Socrates, has taken possession of you all? And why, sillybillies, do you knock under to one another? I say that if you want really to know what justice is, you should not only ask but answer, and you should not seek honour to yourself from the refutation of an opponent, but have your own answer; for there is many a one who can ask and cannot answer. And now I will not have you say that justice is duty or advantage or profit or gain or interest, for this sort of nonsense will not do for me; I must have clearness and accuracy.

I was panic-stricken at his words, and could not look at him without trembling. Indeed I believe that if I had not fixed my eye upon him, I should have been struck dumb: but when I saw his fury rising, I looked at him first, and was therefore able to reply to him.

Thrasymachus, I said, with a quiver, don't be hard upon us. Polemarchus and I may have been guilty of a little mistake in the argument, but I can assure you that the error was not intentional. If we were seeking for a piece of gold, you would not imagine that we were 'knocking under to one another,' and so losing our chance of finding it. And why, when we are seeking for justice, a thing more precious than many pieces of gold, do you say that we are weakly yielding to one another and not doing our utmost to get at the truth? Nay, my good friend, we are most willing and anxious to do so, but the fact is that we cannot. And if so, you people who know all things should pity us and not be angry with us.

How characteristic of Socrates! he replied, with a bitter laugh;—that's your ironical style! Did I not foresee—have I not already told you, that whatever he was asked he would refuse to answer, and try irony or any other shuffle, in order that he might avoid answering?

You are a philosopher, Thrasymachus, I replied, and well know that if you ask a person what numbers make up twelve, taking care to prohibit him whom you ask from answering twice six, or three times four, or six times two, or four times three, 'for this sort of nonsense will not do for me,'—then obviously, if that is your way of putting the question, no one can answer you. But suppose that he were to retort, 'Thrasymachus, what do you mean? If one of these numbers which you interdict be the true answer to the question, am I falsely to say some other number which is not the right one?—is that your meaning?'—How would you answer him?

Just as if the two cases were at all alike! he said.

Why should they not be? I replied; and even if they are not, but only appear to be so to the person who is asked, ought he not to say what he thinks, whether you and I forbid him or not?

I presume then that you are going to make one of the interdicted answers?

I dare say that I may, notwithstanding the danger, if upon reflection I approve of any of them.

But what if I give you an answer about justice other and better, he said, than any of these? What do you deserve to have done to you?

Done to me!—as becomes the ignorant, I must learn from the wise—that is what I deserve to have done to me.

What, and no payment! a pleasant notion!

I will pay when I have the money, I replied.

But you have, Socrates, said Glaucon: and you, Thrasymachus, need be under no anxiety about money, for we will all make a contribution for Socrates.

Yes, he replied, and then Socrates will do as he always does—refuse to answer himself, but take and pull to pieces the answer of some one else.

Why, my good friend, I said, how can any one answer who knows, and says that he knows, just nothing; and who even if he has some faint notions of his own, is told by a man of authority not to utter them? The natural thing is that the speaker should be some one like yourself who professes to know and can tell what he knows. Will you then kindly answer, for the edification of the company and of myself?

Glaucon and the rest of the company joined in my request and Thrasymachus, as any one might see, was in reality eager to speak; for he thought that he had an excellent answer, and would distinguish himself. But at first he affected to insist on my answering; at length he consented to begin. Behold, he said, the wisdom of Socrates; he refuses to teach himself, and goes about learning of others, to whom he never even says Thank you.

That I learn of others, I replied, is quite true; but that I am ungrateful I wholly deny. Money I have none, and therefore I pay in praise, which is all I have; and how ready I am to praise any one who appears to me to speak well you will very soon find out when you answer; for I expect that you will answer well.

Listen, then, he said; I proclaim that justice is nothing else than the interest of the stronger. And now why do you not praise me? But of course you won't.

Let me first understand you, I replied. Justice, as you say, is the interest of the stronger. What, Thrasymachus, is the meaning of this? You cannot mean to say that because Polydamas, the pancratiast, is stronger than we are, and finds the eating of beef conducive to his bodily strength, that to eat beef is therefore equally for our good who are weaker than he is, and right and just for us?

That's abominable of you, Socrates; you take the words in the sense which is most damaging to the argument.

Not at all, my good sir, I said; I am trying to understand them; and I wish that you would be a little clearer.

Well, he said, have you never heard that forms of government differ; there are tyrannies, and there are democracies, and there are aristocracies?

Yes, I know.

And the government is the ruling power in each state?

Certainly.

And the different forms of government make laws democratical, aristocratical, tyrannical, with a view to their several interests; and these laws, which are made by them for their own interests, are the justice which they deliver to their subjects, and him who transgresses them they punish as a breaker of the law, and unjust. And that is what I mean when I say that in all states there is the same principle of justice, which is the interest of the government; and as the government must be supposed to have power, the only reasonable conclusion is, that everywhere there is one principle of justice, which is the interest of the stronger.

Now I understand you, I said; and whether you are right or not I will try to discover. But let me remark, that in defining justice you have yourself used the word 'interest' which you forbade me to use. It is true, however, that in your definition the words 'of the stronger' are added.

A small addition, you must allow, he said.

Great or small, never mind about that: we must first enquire whether what you are saying is the truth. Now we are both agreed that justice is interest of some sort, but you go on to say 'of the stronger'; about this addition I am not so sure, and must therefore consider further.

Proceed.

I will; and first tell me, Do you admit that it is just for subjects to obey their rulers?

I do.

But are the rulers of states absolutely infallible, or are they sometimes liable to err?

To be sure, he replied, they are liable to err.

Then in making their laws they may sometimes make them rightly, and sometimes not?

True.

When they make them rightly, they make them agreeably to their interest; when they are mistaken, contrary to their interest; you admit that?

Yes.

And the laws which they make must be obeyed by their subjects,— and that is what you call justice?

Doubtless.

Then justice, according to your argument, is not only obedience to the interest of the stronger but the reverse?

What is that you are saying? he asked.

I am only repeating what you are saying, I believe. But let us consider: Have we not admitted that the rulers may be mistaken about their own interest in what they command, and also that to obey them is justice? Has not that been admitted?

Yes.

Then you must also have acknowledged justice not to be for the interest of the stronger, when the rulers unintentionally command things to be done which are to their own injury. For if, as you say, justice is the obedience which the subject renders to their commands, in that case, O wisest of men, is there any escape from the conclusion that the weaker are commanded to do, not what is for the interest, but what is for the injury of the stronger?

Nothing can be clearer, Socrates, said Polemarchus.

Yes, said Cleitophon, interposing, if you are allowed to be his witness.

But there is no need of any witness, said Polemarchus, for Thrasymachus himself acknowledges that rulers may sometimes command what is not for their own interest, and that for subjects to obey them is justice.

Yes, Polemarchus,—Thrasymachus said that for subjects to do what was commanded by their rulers is just.

Yes, Cleitophon, but he also said that justice is the interest of the stronger, and, while admitting both these propositions, he further acknowledged that the stronger may command the weaker who are his subjects to do what is not for his own interest; whence follows that justice is the injury quite as much as the interest of the stronger.

But, said Cleitophon, he meant by the interest of the stronger what the stronger thought to be his interest,—this was what the weaker had to do; and this was affirmed by him to be justice.

Those were not his words, rejoined Polemarchus.

Never mind, I replied, if he now says that they are, let us accept his statement. Tell me, Thrasymachus, I said, did you mean by justice what the stronger thought to be his interest, whether really so or not?

Certainly not, he said. Do you suppose that I call him who is mistaken the stronger at the time when he is mistaken?

Yes, I said, my impression was that you did so, when you admitted that the ruler was not infallible but might be sometimes mistaken.

You argue like an informer, Socrates. Do you mean, for example, that he who is mistaken about the sick is a physician in that he is mistaken? or that he who errs in arithmetic or grammar is an arithmetician or grammarian at the time when he is making the mistake, in respect of the mistake? True, we say that the physician or arithmetician or grammarian has made a mistake, but this is only a way of speaking; for the fact is that neither the grammarian nor any other person of skill ever makes a mistake in so far as he is what his name implies; they none of them err unless their skill fails them, and then they cease to be skilled artists. No artist or sage or ruler errs at the time when he is what his name implies; though he is commonly said to err, and I adopted the common mode of speaking. But to be perfectly accurate, since you are such a lover of accuracy, we should say that the ruler, in so far as he is a ruler, is unerring, and, being unerring, always commands that which is for his own interest; and the subject is required to execute his commands; and therefore, as I said at first and now repeat, justice is the interest of the stronger.

Indeed, Thrasymachus, and do I really appear to you to argue like an informer?

Certainly, he replied.

And do you suppose that I ask these questions with any design of injuring you in the argument?

Nay, he replied, 'suppose' is not the word—I know it; but you will be found out, and by sheer force of argument you will never prevail.

I shall not make the attempt, my dear man; but to avoid any misunderstanding occurring between us in future, let me ask, in what sense do you speak of a ruler or stronger whose interest, as you were saying, he being the superior, it is just that the inferior should execute—is he a ruler in the popular or in the strict sense of the term?

In the strictest of all senses, he said. And now cheat and play the informer if you can; I ask no quarter at your hands. But you never will be able, never.

And do you imagine, I said, that I am such a madman as to try and cheat Thrasymachus? I might as well shave a lion.

Why, he said, you made the attempt a minute ago, and you failed.

Enough, I said, of these civilities. It will be better that I should ask you a question: Is the physician, taken in that strict sense of which you are speaking, a healer of the sick or a maker of money? And remember that I am now speaking of the true physician.

A healer of the sick, he replied.

And the pilot—that is to say, the true pilot—is he a captain of sailors or a mere sailor?

A captain of sailors.

The circumstance that he sails in the ship is not to be taken into account; neither is he to be called a sailor; the name pilot by which he is distinguished has nothing to do with sailing, but is significant of his skills and of his authority over the sailors.

Very true, he said.

Now, I said, every art has an interest?

Certainly.

For which the art has to consider and provide?

Yes, that is the aim of art.

And the interest of any art is the perfection of it—this and nothing else?

What do you mean?

I mean what I may illustrate negatively by the example of the body. Suppose you were to ask me whether the body is self-sufficing or has wants, I should reply: Certainly the body has wants; for the body may be ill and require to be cured, and has therefore interests to which the art of medicine ministers; and this is the origin and intention of medicine, as you will acknowledge. Am I not right?

Quite right, he replied.

But is the art of medicine or any other art faulty or deficient in any quality in the same way that the eye may be deficient in sight or the ear fail of hearing, and therefore requires another art to provide for the interests of seeing and hearing—has art in itself, I say, any similar liability to fault or defect, and does every art require another supplementary art to provide for its interests, and that another and another without end? Or have the arts to look only after their own interests? Or have they no need either of themselves or of another?—having no faults or defects, they have no need to correct them, either by the exercise of their own art or of any other; they have only to consider the interest of their subject-matter. For every art remains pure and faultless while remaining true—that is to say, while perfect and unimpaired. Take the words in your precise sense, and tell me whether I am not right.

Yes, clearly.

Then medicine does not consider the interest of medicine, but the interest of the body?

True, he said.

Nor does the art of horsemanship consider the interests of the art of horsemanship, but the interests of the horse; neither do any other arts care for themselves, for they have no needs; they care only for that which is the subject of their art?

True, he said,

But surely, Thrasymachus, the arts are the superiors and rulers of their own subjects?

To this he assented with a good deal of reluctance.

Then, I said, no science or art considers or enjoins the interest of the stronger or superior, but only the interest of the subject and weaker?

He made an attempt to contest this proposition also, but finally acquiesced.

Then, I continued, no physician, in so far as he is a physician, considers his own good in what he prescribes, but the good of his patient; for the true physician is also a ruler having the human body as a subject, and is not a mere money-maker; that has been admitted?

Yes.

And the pilot likewise, in the strict sense of the term, is a ruler of sailors and not a mere sailor?

That has been admitted.

And such a pilot and ruler will provide and prescribe for the interest of the sailor who is under him, and not for his own or the ruler's interest?

He gave a reluctant 'Yes.'

Then, I said, Thrasymachus, there is no one in any rule who, in so far as he is a ruler, considers or enjoins what is for his own interest, but always what is for the interest of his subject or suitable to his art; to that he looks, and that alone he considers in everything which he says and does.

Book II

(The discussion of book one does not satisfy the disciples of Socrates, and they challenge him to continue the investigation into justice. After deciding they are serious in their request, Socrates—used here as the narrator for Plato's own philosophical purposes—advances the inquiry by posing the theory that justice is alike in cities and in individuals. Plato's great work takes its name from the imagined state that Socrates here begins to create.)

Glaucon and the rest entreated me by all means not to let the questions drop, but to proceed in the investigation. They wanted to arrive at the truth, first, about the nature of justice and injustice, and secondly, about their relative advantages. I told them, what I really thought, that the enquiry would be of a serious nature, and would require very good eyes. Seeing then, I said, that we are no great wits, I think that we had better adopt a method which I may illustrate thus; suppose that a short-sighted person had been asked by some one to read small letters from a distance; and it occurred to some one else that they might be found in another place which was larger and in which the letters were larger—if they were the same and he could read the larger letters first, and then proceed to the lesser—this would have been thought a rare piece of good fortune.

Very true, said Adeimantus; but how does the illustration apply to our enquiry?

I will tell you, I replied; justice, which is the subject of our enquiry, is, as you know, sometimes spoken of as the virtue of an individual, and sometimes as the virtue of a State.

True, he replied.

And is not a State larger than an individual?

It is.

Then in the larger the quantity of justice is likely to be larger and more easily discernible. I propose therefore that we enquire into the nature of justice and injustice, first as they appear in the State, and secondly in the individual, proceeding from the greater to the lesser and comparing them.

That, he said, is an excellent proposal.

And if we imagine the State in process of creation, we shall see the justice and injustice of the State in process of creation also.

I dare say.

When the State is completed there may be a hope that the object of our search will be more easily discovered.

Yes, far more easily.

But ought we to attempt to construct one? I said; for to do so, as I am inclined to think, will be a very serious task. Reflect therefore.

I have reflected, said Adeimantus, and am anxious that you should proceed.

A State, I said, arises, as I conceive, out of the needs of mankind; no one is self-sufficing, but all of us have many wants. Can any other origin of a State be imagined?

There can be no other.

Then, as we have many wants, and many persons are needed to supply them, one takes a helper for one purpose and another for another; and when these partners and helpers are gathered together in one habitation the body of inhabitants is termed a State.

True, he said.

And they exchange with one another, and one gives, and another receives, under the idea that the exchange will be for their good.

Very true.

Then, I said, let us begin and create in idea a State; and yet the true creator is necessity, who is the mother of our invention.

Of course, he replied.

Now the first and greatest of necessities is food, which is the condition of life and existence.

Certainly.

The second is a dwelling, and the third clothing and the like.

True.

And now let us see how our city will be able to supply this great demand: We may suppose that one man is a husbandman, another a builder, some one else a weaver—shall we add to them a shoemaker, or perhaps some other purveyor to our bodily wants?

Quite right.

The barest notion of a State must include four or five men.

Clearly.

And how will they proceed? Will each bring the result of his labours into a common stock?—the individual husbandman, for example, producing for four, and labouring four times as long and as much as he need in the provision of food with which he supplies others as well as himself; or will he have nothing to do with others and not be at the trouble of producing for them, but provide for himself alone a fourth of the food in a fourth of the time, and in the remaining three-fourths of his time be employed in making a house or a coat or a pair of shoes, having no partnership with others, but supplying himself all his own wants?

Adeimantus thought that he should aim at producing food only and not at producing everything.

Probably, I replied, that would be the better way; and when I hear you say this, I am myself reminded that we are not all alike; there are diversities of natures among us which are adapted to different occupations.

Very true.

And will you have a work better done when the workman has many occupations, or when he has only one?

When he has only one.

Further, there can be no doubt that a work is spoilt when not done at the right time?

No doubt.

For business is not disposed to wait until the doer of the business is at leisure; but the doer must follow up what he is dong, and make the business his first object.

He must.

And if so, we must infer that all things are produced more plentifully and easily and of a better quality when one man does one thing which is natural to him and does it at the right time, and leaves other things.

Undoubtedly.

Then more than four citizens will be required; for the husbandman will not make his own plough or mattock, or other implements of agriculture, if they are to be good for anything. Neither will the builder make his tools—and he too needs many; and in like manner the weaver and shoemaker.

True.

Then carpenters, and smiths, and many other artisans, will be sharers in our little State, which is already beginning to grow?

True.

Yet even if we add neatherds, shepherds, and other herdsmen, in order that our husbandmen may have oxen to plough with, and builders as well as husbandmen may have draught cattle, and curriers and weavers fleeces and hides,—still our State will not be very large.

This is true; yet neither will it be a very small State which contains all these.

Then, again, there is the situation of the city—to find a place where nothing need be imported is wellnigh impossible.

Impossible.

Then there must be another class of citizens who will bring the required supply from another city?

There must.

But if the trader goes empty-handed, having nothing which they require who would supply his need, he will come back empty-handed.

That is certain.

And therefore what they produced at home must be not only enough for themselves, but such both in quantity and quality as to accommodate those from whom their wants are supplied.

Very true.

Then more husbandmen and more artisans will be required?

They will.

Not to mention the importers and exporters, who are called merchants?

Yes.

Then we shall want merchants?

We shall.

And if merchandise is to be carried over the sea, skilful sailors will also be needed, and in considerable numbers?

Yes, in considerable numbers.

Then, again, within the city, how will they exchange their productions? To secure an exchange was, as you will remember, one of our principal objects when we formed them into a society and constituted a State.

Clearly they will buy and sell.

Then they will need a market-place, and a money-token for purposes of exchange.

Certainly.

Suppose now that a husbandman, or an artisan, brings some production to market, and he comes at a time when there is no one to exchange with him,—is he to leave his calling and sit idle in the marketplace?

Not at all; he will find people there who, seeing the want, undertake the office of salesmen. In well-ordered states they are commonly those who are the weakest in bodily strength, and therefore of little use for any other purpose; their duty is to be in the market, and to give money in exchange for goods to those who desire to sell and to take money from those who desire to buy.

This want, then, creates a class of retail-traders in our State. Is not 'retailer' the term which is applied to those who sit in the market-place engaged in buying and selling, while those who wander from one city to another are called merchants?

Yes, he said.

And there is another class of servants, who are intellectually hardly on the level of companionship; still they have plenty of bodily strength for labour, which accordingly they sell, and are called, if I do not mistake, hirelings, hire being the name which is given to the price of their labour.

True.

Then hirelings will help to make up our population?

Yes.

And now, Adeimantus, is our State matured and perfected?

I think so.

Where, then, is justice, and where is injustice, and in what part of the State did they spring up?

Probably in the dealings of those citizens with one another. I cannot imagine that they are more likely to be found anywhere else.

I dare say that you are right in your suggestion, I said; we had better think the matter out, and not shrink from the enquiry.

Let us then consider, first of all, what will be their way of life, now that we have thus established them. Will they not produce corn, and wine, and clothes, and shoes, and build houses for themselves? And when they are housed, they will work, in summer, commonly, stripped and barefoot, but in winter substantially clothed and shod. They will feed on barley-meal and flour of wheat, baking and kneading them, making noble cakes and loaves; these they will serve up on a mat of reeds or on clean leaves, themselves reclining the while upon beds strewn with yew or myrtle. And they and their children will feast, drinking of the wine which they have made, wearing garlands on their heads, and hymning the praises of the gods, in happy converse with one another. And they will take care that their families do not exceed their means; having an eye to poverty or war.

But, said Glaucon, interposing, you have not given them a relish to their meal.

True, I replied, I had forgotten; of course they must have a relish—salt, and olives, and cheese, and they will boil roots and herbs such as country people prepare; for a dessert we shall give them figs, and peas, and beans; and they will roast myrtle-berries and acorns at the fire, drinking in moderation. And with such a diet they may be expected to live in peace and health to a good old age, and bequeath a similar life to their children after them.

Yes, Socrates, he said, and if you were providing for a city of pigs, how else would you feed the beasts?

But what would you have, Glaucon? I replied.

Why, he said, you should give them the ordinary conveniences of life. People who are to be comfortable are accustomed to lie on sofas, and dine off tables, and they should have sauces and sweets in the modern style.

Yes, I said, now I understand: the question which you would have me consider is, not only how a State, but how a luxurious State is created; and possibly there is no harm in this, for in such a State we shall be more likely to see how justice and injustice originate. In my opinion the true and healthy constitution of the State is the one which I have described. But if you wish also to see a State at fever-heat, I have no objection. For I suspect the many will not be satisfied with the simpler way of life. They will be for adding sofas, and tables, and other furniture; also dainties, and perfumes, and incense, and courtesans, and cakes, all these not of one sort only, but in every variety; we must go beyond the necessaries of which I was at first speaking, such as houses, and clothes, and shoes: the arts of the painter and the embroiderer will have to be set in motion, and gold and ivory and all sorts of materials must be procured.

True, he said.

Then we must enlarge our borders; for the original healthy State is no longer sufficient. Now will the city have to fill and swell with a multitude of callings which are not required by any natural want; such as the whole tribe of hunters and actors, of whom one large class have to do with forms and colours; another will be the votaries of music— poets and their attendant train of rhapsodists, players, dancers, contractors; also makers of divers kinds of articles, including women's dresses. And we shall want more servants. Will not tutors be also in request, and nurses wet and dry, tirewomen and barbers, as well as confectioners and cooks; and swineherds, too, who were not needed and therefore had no place in the former edition of our State, but are needed now? They must not be forgotten: and there will be animals of many other kinds, if people eat them.

Certainly.

And living in this way we shall have much greater need of physicians than before?

Much greater.

And the country which was enough to support the original inhabitants will be too small now, and not enough?

Quite true.

Then a slice of our neighbours' land will be wanted by us for pasture and tillage, and they will want a slice of ours, if, like ourselves, they exceed the limit of necessity, and give themselves up to the unlimited accumulation of wealth?

That, Socrates, will be inevitable.

And so we shall go to war, Glaucon. Shall we not?

Most certainly, he replied.

Then, without determining as yet whether war does good or harm, thus much we may affirm, that now we have discovered war to be derived from causes which are also the causes of almost all the evils in States, private as well as public.

Undoubtedly.

And our state must once more enlarge; and this time the enlargement will be nothing short of a whole army, which will have to go out and fight with the invaders for all that we have, as well as for the things and persons whom we were describing above.

Why? he said; are they not capable of defending themselves?

No, I said; not if we were right in the principle which was acknowledged by all of us when we were framing the State: the principle, as you will remember, was that one man cannot practise many arts with success.

Very true, he said.

But is not war an art?

Certainly.

An art requiring as much attention as shoemaking?

Quite true.

And the shoemaker was not allowed by us to be a husbandman, or a weaver, or a builder—in order that we might have our shoes well made; but to him and to every other worker was assigned one work for which he was by nature fitted, and at that he was to continue working all his life long and at no other; he was not to let opportunities slip, and then he would become a good workman. Now nothing can be more important than that the work of a soldier should be well done. But is war an art so easily acquired that man may be a warrior who is also a husbandman, or shoemaker, or other artisan; although no one in the world would be a good dice or draught player who merely took up the game as a recreation, and had not from his earliest years devoted himself to this and nothing else? No tools will make a man a skilled workman, or master of defence, nor be of any use to him who has not learned how to handle them, and has never bestowed any attention upon them. How then will he who takes up a shield or other implement of war become a good fighter all in a day, whether with heavy-armed or any other kind of troops?

Yes, he said, the tools which would teach men their own use would be beyond price.

And the higher the duties of the guardian, I said, the more time, and skill, and art, and application will be needed by him?

No doubt, he replied.

Will he not also require natural aptitude for his calling?

Certainly.

Then it will be our duty to select, if we can, natures which are fitted for the task or guarding the city?

It will.

And the selection will be no easy matter, I said; but we must be brave and do our best.

We must.

Is not the noble youth very like a well-bred dog in respect of guarding and watching?

What do you mean?

I mean that both of them ought to be quick to see, and swift to overtake the enemy when they see him; and strong too if, when they have caught him, they have to fight with him.

All these qualities, he replied, will certainly be required by them.

Well, and your guardian must be brave if he is to fight well?

Certainly.

And is he likely to be brave who has no spirit, whether horse or dog or any other animal? Have you never observed how invincible and unconquerable is spirit and how the presence of it makes the soul of any creature to be absolutely fearless and indomitable?

I have.

Then now we have a clear notion of the bodily qualities which are required in the guardian.

True.

And also of the mental ones; his soul is to be full of spirit?

Yes.

But are not these spirited natures apt to be savage with one another, and with everybody else?

A difficulty by no means easy to overcome, he replied.

Whereas, I said, they ought to be dangerous to their enemies, and gentle to their friends; if not, they will destroy themselves without waiting for their enemies to destroy them.

True, he said.

What is to be done then? I said; how shall we find a gentle nature which has also a great spirit, for the one is the contradiction of the other?

True.

He will not be a good guardian who is wanting in either of these two qualities; and yet the combination of them appears to be impossible; and hence we must infer that to be a good guardian is impossible.

I am afraid that what you say is true, he replied.

Here feeling perplexed I began to think over what had preceded.— My friend I said, no wonder that we are in a perplexity; for we have lost sight of the image which we had before us.

What do you mean? he said.

I mean to say that there do exist natures gifted with those opposite qualities.

And where do you find them?

Many animals, I replied, furnish examples of them; our friend the dog is a very good one: you know that well-bred dogs are perfectly gentle to their families and acquaintances, and the reverse to strangers.

Yes, I know.

Then there is nothing impossible or out of the order of nature in our finding a guardian who has a similar combination of qualities?

Certainly not.

Would not he who is fitted to be a guardian, besides the spirited nature, need to have the qualities of a philosopher?

I do not apprehend your meaning.

The trait of which I am speaking, I replied, may be also seen in the dog, and is remarkable in the animal.

What trait?

Why, a dog, whenever he sees a stranger, is angry; when an acquaintance, he welcomes him, although the one has never done him any harm, nor the other any good. Did this never strike you as curious?

The matter never struck me before; but I quite recognise the truth of your remark.

And surely this instinct of the dog is very charming;—your dog is a true philosopher.

Why?

Why, because he distinguishes the face of friend and of an enemy only by the criterion of knowing and not knowing. And must not an animal be a lover of learning who determines what he likes and dislikes by the test of knowledge and ignorance?

Most assuredly.

And is not the love of learning the love of wisdom, which is philosophy?

They are the same, he replied.

And may we not say confidently of man also, that he who is likely to be gentle to his friends and acquaintances, must by nature be a lover of wisdom and knowledge?

That we may safely affirm.

Then he who is to be a really good and noble guardian of the State will require to unite in himself philosophy and spirit and swiftness and strength?

Undoubtedly.

Then we have found the desired natures; and now that we have found them, how are they to be reared and educated? Is not this an enquiry which may be expected to throw light on the greater enquiry which is our final end—How do justice and injustice grow up in States? for we do not want either to omit what is to the point or to draw out the argument to an inconvenient length.

Adeimantus thought that the enquiry would be of great service to us.

Then, I said, my dear friend, the task must not be given up, even if somewhat long.

Certainly not.

Come then, and let us pass a leisure hour in story-telling, and our story shall be the education of our heroes.

By all means.

And what shall be their education? Can we find a better than the traditional sort?—and this has two divisions, gymnastic for the body, and music for the soul.

True.

Shall we begin education with music, and go on to gymnastic afterwards?

By all means.

And when you speak of music, do you include literature or not?

I do.

And literature may be either true or false?

Yes.

And the young should be trained in both kinds, and we begin with the false?

I do not understand your meaning, he said.

You know, I said, that we begin by telling children stories which, though not wholly destitute of truth, are in the main fictitious; and these stories are told them when they are not of an age to learn gymnastics.

Very true.

That was my meaning when I said that we must teach music before gymnastics.

Quite right, he said.

You know also that the beginning is the most important part of any work, especially in the case of a young and tender thing; for that is the time at which the character is being formed and the desired impression is more readily taken.

Quite true.

And shall we just carelessly allow children to hear any casual tales which may be devised by casual persons, and to receive into their minds ideas for the most part the very opposite of those which we should wish them to have when they are grown up?

We cannot.

Then the first thing will be to establish a censorship of the writers of fiction, and let the censors receive any tale of fiction which is good, and reject the bad; and we will desire mothers and nurses to tell their children the authorised ones only. Let them fashion the mind with such tales, even more fondly than they mould the body with their hands; but most of those which are now in use must be discarded.

Book IV

(Book four brings the comparison of the state with the individual to a preliminary conclusion as Plato—through Socrates—makes his case that the tri-partite soul is the just equivalent of the harmonious state.)

Let us push on.

Here I saw something: Halloo! I said, I begin to perceive a track, and I believe that the quarry will not escape.

Good news, he said.

Truly, I said, we are stupid fellows.

Why so?

Why, my good sir, at the beginning of our enquiry, ages ago, there was justice tumbling out at our feet, and we never saw her; nothing could be more ridiculous. Like people who go about looking for what they have in their hands—that was the way with us—we looked not at what we were seeking, but at what was far off in the distance; and therefore, I suppose, we missed her.

What do you mean?

I mean to say that in reality for a long time past we have been talking of justice, and have failed to recognise her.

I grow impatient at the length of your exordium.

Well then, tell me, I said, whether I am right or not: You remember the original principle which we were always laying down at the foundation of the State, that one man should practise one thing only, the thing to which his nature was best adapted;—now justice is this principle or a part of it.

Yes, we often said that one man should do one thing only.

Further, we affirmed that justice was doing one's own business, and not being a busybody; we said so again and again, and many others have said the same to us.

Yes, we said so.

Then to do one's own business in a certain way may be assumed to be justice. Can you tell me whence I derive this inference?

I cannot, but I should like to be told.

Because I think that this is the only virtue which remains in the State when the other virtues of temperance and courage and wisdom are abstracted; and, that this is the ultimate cause and condition of the existence of all of them, and while remaining in them is also their preservative; and we were saying that if the three were discovered by us, justice would be the fourth or remaining one.

That follows of necessity.

If we are asked to determine which of these four qualities by its presence contributes most to the excellence of the State, whether the agreement of rulers and subjects, or the preservation in the soldiers of the opinion which the law ordains about the true nature of dangers, or wisdom and watchfulness in the rulers, or whether this other which I am mentioning, and which is found in children and women, slave and freeman, artisan, ruler, subject,—the quality, I mean, of every one doing his own work, and not being a busybody, would claim the palm—the question is not so easily answered.

Certainly, he replied, there would be a difficulty in saying which.

Then the power of each individual in the State to do his own work appears to compete with the other political virtues, wisdom, temperance, courage.

Yes, he said.

And the virtue which enters into this competition is justice?

Exactly.

Let us look at the question from another point of view: Are not the rulers in a State those to whom you would entrust the office of determining suits at law?

Certainly.

And are suits decided on any other ground but that a man may neither take what is another's, nor be deprived of what is his own?

Yes; that is their principle.

Which is a just principle.

Yes.

Then on this view also justice will be admitted to be the having and doing what is a man's own, and belongs to him?

Very true.

Think, now, and say whether you agree with me or not. Suppose a carpenter to be doing the business of a cobbler, or a cobbler of a carpenter; and suppose them to exchange their implements or their duties, or the same person to be doing the work of both, or whatever be the change; do you think that any great harm would result to the State?

Not much.

But when the cobbler or any other man whom nature designed to be a trader, having his heart lifted up by wealth or strength or the number of his followers, or any like advantage, attempts to force his way into the class of warriors, or a warrior into that of legislators and guardians, for which he is unfitted, and either to take the implements or the duties of the other; or when one man is trader, legislator, and warrior all in one, then I think you will agree with me in saying that this interchange and this meddling of one with another is the ruin of the State.

Most true.

Seeing then, I said, that there are three distinct classes, any meddling of one with another, or the change of one into another, is the greatest harm to the State, and may be most justly termed evil-doing?

Precisely.

And the greatest degree of evil-doing to one's own city would be termed by you injustice?

Certainly.

This then is injustice; and on the other hand when the trader, the auxiliary, and the guardian each do their own business, that is justice, and will make the city just.

I agree with you.

We will not, I said, be over-positive as yet; but if, on trial, this conception of justice be verified in the individual as well as in the State, there will be no longer any room for doubt; if it be not verified, we must have a fresh enquiry. First let us complete the old investigation, which we began, as you remember, under the impression that, if we could previously examine justice on the larger scale, there would be less difficulty in discerning her in the individual. That larger example appeared to be the State, and accordingly we constructed as good a one as we could, knowing well that in the good State justice would be found. Let the discovery which we made be now applied to the individual—if they agree, we shall be satisfied; or, if there be a difference in the individual, we will come back to the State and have another trial of the theory. The friction of the two when rubbed together may possibly strike a light in which justice will shine forth, and the vision which is then revealed we will fix in our souls.

That will be in regular course; let us do as you say.

I proceeded to ask: When two things, a greater and less, are called by the same name, are they like or unlike in so far as they are called the same?

Like, he replied.

The just man then, if we regard the idea of justice only, will be like the just State?

He will.

And a State was thought by us to be just when the three classes in the State severally did their own business; and also thought to be temperate and valiant and wise by reason of certain other affections and qualities of these same classes?

True, he said.

And so of the individual; we may assume that he has the same three principles in his own soul which are found in the State; and he may be rightly described in the same terms, because he is affected in the same manner?

Certainly, he said.

Once more then, O my friend, we have alighted upon an easy question—whether the soul has these three principles or not?

An easy question! Nay, rather, Socrates, the proverb holds that hard is the good.

Very true, I said; and I do not think that the method which we are employing is at all adequate to the accurate solution of this question; the true method is another and a longer one. Still we may arrive at a solution not below the level of the previous enquiry.

May we not be satisfied with that? he said;—under the circumstances, I am quite content.

I too, I replied, shall be extremely well satisfied.

Then faint not in pursuing the speculation, he said.

Must we not acknowledge, I said, that in each of us there are the same principles and habits which there are in the State; and that from the individual they pass into the State?—how else can they come there? Take the quality of passion or spirit;—it would be ridiculous to imagine that this quality, when found in States, is not derived from the individuals who are supposed to possess it, *e.g.,* the Thracians, Scythians, and in general the northern nations; and the same may be said of the love of knowledge, which is the special characteristic of our part of the world, or of the love of money, which may, with equal truth, be attributed to the Phoenicians and Egyptians.

Exactly so, he said.

There is no difficulty in understanding this.

None whatever.

But the question is not quite so easy when we proceed to ask whether these principles are three or one; whether, that is to say, we learn with one part of our nature, are angry with another, and with a third part desire the satisfaction of our natural appetites; or whether the whole soul comes into play in each sort of action—to determine that is the difficulty.

Yes, he said; there lies the difficulty.

Then let us now try and determine whether they are the same or different.

How can we? he asked.

I replied as follows: The same thing clearly cannot act or be acted upon in the same part or in relation to the same thing at the same time, in contrary ways; and therefore whenever this contradiction occurs in things apparently the same, we know that they are really not the same, but different.

Good.

For example, I said, can the same thing be at rest and in motion at the same time in the same part?

Impossible.

Still, I said, let us have a more precise statement of terms, lest we should hereafter fall out by the way. Imagine the case of a man who is standing and also moving his hands and his head, and suppose a person to say that one and the same person is in motion and at rest at the same moment—to such a mode of speech we should object, and should rather say that one part of him is in motion while another is at rest.

Very true.

And suppose the objector to refine still further, and to draw the nice distinction that not only parts of tops, but whole tops, when they spin round with their pegs fixed on the spot, are at rest and in motion at the same time (and he may say the same of anything which revolves in the same spot), his objection would not be admitted by us, because in such cases things are not at rest and in motion in the same parts of themselves; we should rather say that they have both an axis and a circumference; and that the axis stands still, for there is no deviation from the perpendicular; and that the circumference goes round. But if, while revolving, the axis inclines either to the right or left, forwards or backwards, then in no point of view can they be at rest.

That is the correct mode of describing them, he replied.

Then none of these objections will confuse us, or incline us to believe that the same thing at the same time, in the same part or in relation to the same thing, can act or be acted upon in contrary ways.

Certainly not, according to my way of thinking.

Yet, I said, that we may not be compelled to examine all such objections, and prove at length that they are untrue, let us assume their absurdity, and go forward on the understanding that hereafter, if this assumption turn out to be untrue, all the consequences which follow shall be withdrawn.

Yes, he said, that will be the best way.

Well, I said, would you not allow that assent and dissent, desire and aversion, attraction and repulsion, are all of them opposites, whether they are regarded as active or passive (for that makes no difference in the fact of their opposition)?

Yes, he said, they are opposites.

Well, I said, and hunger and thirst, and the desires in general, and again willing and wishing,--all these you would refer to the classes already mentioned. You would say—would you not?—that the soul of him who desires is seeking after the object of his desires; or that he is drawing to himself the thing which he wishes to possess: or again, when a person wants anything to be given him, his mind, longing for the realization of his desires, intimates his wish to have it by a nod of assent, as if he had been asked a question?

Very true.

And what would you say of unwillingness and dislike and the absence of desire; should not these be referred to the opposite class of repulsion and rejection?

Certainly.

Admitting this to be true of desire generally, let us suppose a particular class of desires, and out of these we will select hunger and thirst, as they are termed, which are the most obvious of them?

Let us take that class, he said.

The object of one is food, and of the other drink?

Yes.

And here comes the point: is not thirst the desire which the soul has of drink, and of drink only; not of drink qualified by anything else; for example, warm or cold, or much or little, or, in a word, drink of any particular sort: but if the thirst is accompanied by heat, then the desire is of cold drink; or, if accompanied by cold, then of warm drink; or, if the thirst be excessive, then the drink which is desired will be excessive; or, if not great, the quantity of drink will also be small: but thirst pure and simple will desire drink pure and simple, which is the natural satisfaction of thirst, as food is of hunger?

Yes, he said; the simple desire is, as you say, in every case of the simple object, and the qualified desire of the qualified object.

But here a confusion may arise; and I should wish to guard against an opponent starting up and saying that no man desires drink only, but good drink, or food only, but good food; for good is the universal object of desire, and thirst being a desire, will necessarily be thirst after good drink; and the same is true of every other desire.

Yes, he replied, the opponent might have something to say.

Nevertheless I should still maintain, that of relatives some have a quality attached to either term of the relation; others are simple and have their correlatives simple.

I do not know what you mean.

Well, you know of course that the greater is relative to the less?

Certainly.

And the much greater to the much less?

Yes.

And the sometime greater to be the sometime less, and the greater that is to be to the less that is to be?

Certainly, he said.

And so of more and less, and of other correlative terms, such as the double and the half, or again, the heavier and the lighter, the swifter and the slower; and of hot and cold, and of any other relatives;—is not this true of all of them?

Yes.

And does not the same principle hold in the sciences? The object of science is knowledge (assuming that to be the true definition), but the object of a particular science is a particular kind of knowledge; I mean, for example, that the science of house-building is a kind of knowledge which is defined and distinguished from other kinds and is therefore termed architecture.

Certainly.

Because it has a particular quality which no other has?

Yes.

And it has this particular quality because it has an object of a particular kind; and this is true of the other arts and sciences?

Yes.

Now, then, if I have made myself clear, you will understand my original meaning in what I said about relatives. My meaning was, that if one term of a relation is taken alone, the other is taken alone; if one term is qualified, the other is also qualified. I do not mean to say that relatives may not be disparate, or that the science of health is healthy, or of disease necessarily diseased, or that the sciences of good and evil are therefore good and evil; but only that, when the term science is no longer used absolutely, but has a qualified object which in this case is the nature of health and disease, it becomes defined, and is hence called not merely science, but the science of medicine.

I quite understand, and I think as you do.

Would you not say that thirst is one of these essentially relative terms, having clearly a relation—

Yes, thirst is relative to drink.

And a certain kind of thirst is relative to a certain kind of drink; but thirst taken alone is neither much nor little, nor of good nor bad, nor of any particular kind of drink, but of drink only?

Certainly.

Then the soul of the thirsty one, in so far as he is thirsty, desires only drink; for this he yearns and tries to obtain it?

That is plain.

And if you suppose something which pulls a thirsty soul away from drink, that must be different from the thirsty principle which draws him like a beast to drink; for, as we were saying, the same thing cannot at the same time with the same part of itself act in contrary ways about the same.

Impossible.

No more than you can say that the hands of the archer push and pull the bow at the same time, but what you say is that one hand pushes and the other pulls.

Exactly so, he replied.

And might a man be thirsty, and yet unwilling to drink?

Yes, he said, it constantly happens.

And in such a case what is one to say? Would you not say that there was something in the soul bidding a man to drink, and something else forbidding him, which is other and stronger than the principle which bids him?

I should say so.

And the forbidding principles derived from reason, and that which bids and attracts proceeds from passion and disease?

Clearly.

Then we may fairly assume that they are two, and that they differ from one another; the one with which a man reasons, we may call the rational principle of the soul, the other, with which he loves and hungers and thirsts and feels the flutterings of any other desire, may be termed the irrational or appetitive, the ally of sundry pleasures and satisfactions?

Yes, he said, we may fairly assume them to be different.

Then let us finally determine that there are two principles existing in the soul. And what of passion, or spirit? Is it a third, or akin to one of the preceding?

I should be inclined to say—akin to desire.

Well, I said, there is a story which I remember to have heard, and in which I put faith. The story is, that Leontius, the son of Aglaion, coming up one day from the Piraeus, under the north wall on the outside, observed some dead bodies lying on the ground at the place of execution. He felt a desire to see them, and also a dread and abhorrence of them; for a time he struggled and covered his eyes, but at length the desire got the better of him; and forcing them open, he ran up to the dead bodies, saying, Look, ye wretches, take your fill of their fair sight.

I have heard the story myself, he said.

The moral of the tale is, that anger at times goes to war with desire, as though they were two distinct things.

Yes; that is the meaning, he said.

And are there not many other cases in which we observe that when a man's desires violently prevail over his reason, he reviles himself, and is angry at the violence within him, and that in this struggle, which is like the struggle of factions in a State, his spirit is on the side of his reason;—but for the passionate or spirited element to take part with the desires when reason decides that she should not be opposed, is a sort of thing which I believe that you never observed occurring in yourself, nor, as I should imagine, in any one else?

Certainly not.

Suppose that a man thinks he has done a wrong to another, the nobler he is the less able is he to feel indignant at any suffering, such as hunger, or cold, or any other pain which the injured person may inflict upon him—these he deems to be just, and, as I say, his anger refuses to be excited by them.

True, he said.

But when he thinks that he is the sufferer of the wrong, then he boils and chafes, and is on the side of what he believes to be justice; and because he suffers hunger or cold or other pain he is only the more determined to persevere and conquer. His noble spirit will not be quelled until he either slays or is slain; or until he hears the voice of the shepherd, that is, reason, bidding his dog bark no more.

The illustration is perfect, he replied; and in our State, as we were saying, the auxiliaries were to be dogs, and to hear the voice of the rulers, who are their shepherds.

I perceive, I said, that you quite understand me; there is, however, a further point which I wish you to consider.

What point?

You remember that passion or spirit appeared at first sight to be a kind of desire, but now we should say quite the contrary; for in the conflict of the soul spirit is arrayed on the side of the rational principle.

Most assuredly.

But a further question arises: Is passion different from reason also, or only a kind of reason; in which latter case, instead of three principles in the soul, there will only be two, the rational and the concupiscent; or rather, as the State was composed of three classes, traders, auxiliaries, counsellors, so may there not be in the individual soul a third element which is passion or spirit, and when not corrupted by bad education is the natural auxiliary of reason?

Yes, he said, there must be a third.

Yes, I replied, if passion, which has already been shown to be different from desire, turn out also to be different from reason.

But that is easily proved:—We may observe even in young children that they are full of spirit almost as soon as they are born. Whereas some of them never seem to attain to the use of reason, and most of them late enough.

Excellent, I said, and you may see passion equally in brute animals, which is a further proof of the truth of what you are saying. And we may once more appeal to the words of Homer, which have been already quoted by us,

'He smote his breast, and thus rebuked his soul;'

for in this verse Homer has clearly supposed the power which reasons about the better and worse to be different from the unreasoning anger which is rebuked by it.

Very true, he said.

And so, after much tossing, we have reached land, and are fairly agreed that the same principles which exist in the State exist also in the individual, and that they are three in number.

Exactly.

Must we not then infer that the individual is wise in the same way, and in virtue of the same quality which makes the State wise?

Certainly.

Also that the same quality which constitutes courage in the State constitutes courage in the individual, and that both the State and the individual bear the same relation to all the other virtues?

Assuredly.

And the individual will be acknowledged by us to be just in the same way in which the State is just?

That follows of course.

We cannot but remember that the justice of the State consisted in each of the three classes doing the work of its own class?

We are not very likely to have forgotten, he said.

We must recollect that the individual in whom the several qualities of his nature do their own work will be just, and will do his own work?

Yes, he said, we must remember that too.

And ought not the rational principle, which is wise, and has the care of the whole soul, to rule, and the passionate or spirited principle to be the subject and ally?

Certainly.

And, as we were saying, the united influence of music and gymnastic will bring them into accord, nerving and sustaining the reason with noble words and lessons, and moderating and soothing and civilizing the wildness of passion by harmony and rhythm?

Quite true, he said.

And these two, thus nurtured and educated, and having learned truly to know their own functions, will rule over the concupiscent, which in each of us is the largest part of the soul and by nature most insatiable of gain; over this they will keep guard, lest, waxing great and strong with the fulness of bodily pleasures, as they are termed, the concupiscent soul, no longer confined to her own sphere, should attempt to enslave and rule those who are not her natural-born subjects, and overturn the whole life of man?

Very true, he said.

Both together will they not be the best defenders of the whole soul and the whole body against attacks from without; the one counselling, and the other fighting under his leader, and courageously executing his commands and counsels?

True.

And he is to be deemed courageous whose spirit retains in pleasure and in pain the commands of reason about what he ought or ought not to fear?

Right, he replied.

And him we call wise who has in him that little part which rules, and which proclaims these commands; that part too being supposed to have a knowledge of what is for the interest of each of the three parts and of the whole?

Assuredly.

And would you not say that he is temperate who has the same elements in friendly harmony, in whom the one ruling principle of reason, and the two subject ones of spirit and desire are equally agreed that reason ought to rule, and do not rebel?

Certainly, he said, that is the true account of temperance whether in the State or individual.

And surely, I said, we have explained again and again how and by virtue of what quality a man will be just.

That is very certain.

And is justice dimmer in the individual, and is her form different, or is she the same which we found her to be in the State?

There is no difference in my opinion, he said.

Because, if any doubt is still lingering in our minds, a few commonplace instances will satisfy us of the truth of what I am saying.

What sort of instances do you mean?

If the case is put to us, must we not admit that the just State, or the man who is trained in the principles of such a State, will be less likely than the unjust to make away with a deposit of gold or silver? Would any one deny this?

No one, he replied.

Will the just man or citizen ever be guilty of sacrilege or theft, or treachery either to his friends or to his country?

Never.

Neither will he ever break faith where there have been oaths or agreements?

Impossible.

No one will be less likely to commit adultery, or to dishonor his father and mother, or to fail in his religious duties?

No one.

And the reason is that each part of him is doing its own business, whether in ruling or being ruled?

Exactly so.

Are you satisfied then that the quality which makes such men and such states is justice, or do you hope to discover some other?

Not I, indeed.

Then our dream has been realized; and the suspicion which we entertained at the beginning of our work of construction, that some divine power must have conducted us to a primary form of justice, has now been verified?

Yes, certainly.

And the division of labour which required the carpenter and the shoemaker and the rest of the citizens to be doing each his own business, and not another's, was a shadow of justice, and for that reason it was of use?

Clearly.

But in reality justice was such as we were describing, being concerned however, not with the outward man, but with the inward, which is the true self and concernment of man: for the just man does not permit the several elements within him to interfere with one another, or any of them to do the work of others,—he sets in order his own inner life, and is his own master and his own law, and at peace with himself; and when he has bound together the three principles within him, which may be compared to the higher, lower, and middle notes of the scale, and the intermediate intervals—when he has bound all these together, and is no longer many, but has become one entirely temperate and perfectly adjusted nature, then he proceeds to act, if he has to act, whether in a matter of property, or in the treatment of the body, or in some affair of politics or private business; always thinking and calling that which preserves and co-operates with this harmonious condition, just and good action, and the knowledge which presides over it, wisdom, and that which at any time impairs this condition, he will call unjust action, and the opinion which presides over it ignorance.

You have said the exact truth, Socrates.

Very good; and if we were to affirm that we had discovered the just man and the just State, and the nature of justice in each of them, we should not be telling a falsehood?

Most certainly not.

May we say so, then?

Let us say so.

Book VII

(Probably the most famous short passage from The Republic, the beginning of book seven presents the myth of the cave, in which Plato distinguishes between the unenlightened and the enlightened soul.)

And now, I said, let me show in a figure how far our nature is enlightened or unenlightened:—Behold! human beings living in an underground den, which has a mouth open towards the light and reaching all along the den; here they have been from their childhood, and have their legs and necks chained so that they cannot move, and can only see before them, being prevented by the chains from turning round their heads. Above and behind them a fire is blazing at a distance, and between the fire and the prisoners there is a raised way; and you will see, if you look, a low wall built along the way, like the screen which marionette players have in front of them, over which they show the puppets.

I see.

And do you see, I said, men passing along the wall carrying all sorts of vessels, and statues and figures of animals made of wood and stone and various materials, which appear over the wall? Some of them are talking, others silent.

You have shown me a strange image, and they are strange prisoners.

Like ourselves, I replied; and they see only their own shadows, or the shadows of one another, which the fire throws on the opposite wall of the cave?

True, he said; how could they see anything but the shadows if they were never allowed to move their heads?

And of the objects which are being carried in like manner they would only see the shadows?

Yes, he said.

And if they were able to converse with one another, would they not suppose that they were naming what was actually before them?

Very true.

And suppose further that the prison had an echo which came from the other side, would they not be sure to fancy when one of the passers-by spoke that the voice which they heard came from the passing shadow?

No question, he replied.

To them, I said, the truth would be literally nothing but the shadows of the images.

That is certain.

And now look again, and see what will naturally follow if the prisoners are released and disabused of their error. At first, when any of them is liberated and compelled suddenly to stand up and turn his neck around and walk and look towards the light, he will suffer sharp pains; the glare will distress him, and he will be unable to see the realities of which in his former state he had seen the shadows; and then conceive some one saying to him, that what he saw before was an illusion, but that now, when he is approaching nearer to being and his eye is turned towards more real existence, he has a clearer vision,—what will be his reply? And you may further imagine that his instructor is pointing to the objects as they pass and requiring him to name them,—will he not be perplexed? Will he not fancy that the shadows which he formerly saw are truer than the objects which are now shown to him?

Far truer.

And if he is compelled to look straight at the light, will he not have a pain in his eyes which will make him turn away to take refuge in the objects of vision which he can see, and which he will conceive to be in reality clearer than the things which are now being shown to him?

True, he said.

And suppose once more, that he is reluctantly dragged up a steep and rugged ascent, and held fast until he is forced into the presence of the sun himself, is he not likely to be pained and irritated? When he approaches the light his eyes will be dazzled, and he will not be able to see anything at all of what are now called realities.

Not all in a moment, he said.

He will require to grow accustomed to the sight of the upper world. And first he will see the shadows best, next the reflections of men and other objects in the water, and then the objects themselves; then he will gaze upon the light of the moon and the stars and the spangled heaven; and he will see the sky and the stars by night better than the sun or the light of the sun by day?

Certainly.

Last of all he will be able to see the sun, and not mere reflections of him in the water, but he will see him in his own proper place, and not in another; and he will contemplate him as he is.

Certainly.

He will then proceed to argue that this is he who gives the seasons and the years, and is the guardian of all that is in the visible world, and in a certain way the cause of all things which he and his fellows have been accustomed to behold?

Clearly, he said, he would first see the sun and then reason about him.

And when he remembered his old habitation, and the wisdom of the den and his fellow-prisoners, do you not suppose that he would felicitate himself on the change, and pity them?

Certainly, he would.

And if they were in the habit of conferring honours among themselves on those who were quickest to observe the passing shadows and to remark which of them went before, and which followed after, and which were together; and who were therefore best able to draw conclusions as to the future, do you think that he would care for such honours and glories, or envy the possessors of them? Would he not say with Homer,

> 'Better to be the poor servant of a poor master,'

and to endure anything, rather than think as they do and live after their manner?

Yes, he said, I think that he would rather suffer anything than entertain these false notions and live in this miserable manner.

Imagine once more, I said, such an one coming suddenly out of the sun to be replaced in his old situation; would he not be certain to have his eyes full of darkness?

To be sure, he said.

And if there were a contest, and he had to compete in measuring the shadows with the prisoners who had never moved out of the den, while his sight was still weak, and before his eyes had become steady (and the time which would be needed to acquire this new habit of sight might be very considerable), would he not be ridiculous? Men would say of him that up he went and down he came without his eyes; and that it was better not even to think of ascending; and if any one tried to loose another and lead him up to the light, let them only catch the offender, and they would put him to death.

No question, he said.

This entire allegory, I said, you may now append, dear Glaucon, to the previous argument; the prison-house is the world of sight, the light of the fire is the sun, and you will not misapprehend me if you interpret the journey upwards to be the ascent of the soul into the intellectual world according to my poor belief, which, at your desire, I have expressed—whether rightly or wrongly God knows. But, whether true or false, my opinion is that in the world of knowledge the idea of good appears last of all, and is seen only with an effort; and, when seen, is also inferred to be the universal author of all things beautiful and right, parent of light and of the lord of light in this visible world, and the immediate source of reason and truth in the intellectual; and that this is the power upon which he who would act rationally either in public or private life must have his eye fixed.

I agree, he said, as far as I am able to understand you.

Moreover, I said, you must not wonder that those who attain to this beatific vision are unwilling to descend to human affairs; for their souls are ever hastening into the upper world where they desire to dwell; which desire of theirs is very natural, if our allegory may be trusted.

ARISTOTLE

(384-322)

"Presumably, however, to say that happiness is the chief good seems a platitude, and a clearer account of what it is is still desired. This might perhaps be given if we could first ascertain the function of man."

Aristotle, the student of Plato at the Academy as Plato was the student of Socrates on the streets and in the gathering places of Athens, completes the great triumvirate of classical Greek philosophy. In contrast to Plato's transcendent idealism Aristotle established himself as the philosopher of common sense, offering a more empirical view of human action and aspiration.

Macedonian by birth, Aristotle returned to his homeland as a tutor to the young heir who would become Alexander the Great. After almost three years Aristotle went again to Athens to found his own school, the Lyceum, and to produce treatises on a remarkable range of subjects, including physics, politics, poetics, psychology, and ethics.

In the *Nicomachean Ethics* he examines human purpose and the means by which those purposes are achieved.

NICOMACHEAN ETHICS

ARISTOTLE

Book I – The Good for Man

Every art and every inquiry, and similarly every action and pursuit, is thought to aim at some good; and for this reason the good has rightly been declared to be that at which all things aim. But a certain difference is found among ends; some are activities, others are products apart from the activities that produce them. Where there are ends apart from the actions, it is the nature of the products to be better than the activities. Now, as there are many actions, arts, and sciences, their ends also are many; the end of the medical art is health, that of shipbuilding a vessel, that of strategy victory, that of economics wealth. But where such arts fall under a single capacity—as bridle-making and the other arts concerned with the equipment of horses fall under the art of riding, and this and every military action under strategy, in the same way other arts fall under yet others—in all of these the ends of the master arts are to be preferred to all the subordinate ends; for it is for the sake of the former that the latter be pursued. It makes no difference whether the activities themselves are the ends of the actions, or something else apart from the activities, as in the case of the sciences just mentioned.

If, then, there is some end of the things we do, which we desire for its own sake (everything else being desired for the sake of this), and if we do not choose everything for the sake of something else (for at that rate the process would go on to infinity, so that our desire would be empty and vain), clearly this must be the good and the chief good. Will not the knowledge of it, then, have a great influence on life? Shall we not, like archers who have a mark to aim at, be more likely to hit upon what is right? If so, we must try, in outline at least to determine what it is, and of which of the sciences or capacities it is the object. It would seem to belong to the most authoritative art and that which is most truly the master art. And politics appears to be of this nature; for it is this that ordains which of the sciences should be studied in a state, and which each class of citizens should learn and up to what point they should learn them; and we see even the most highly esteemed of capacities to fall under this, e.g. strategy, economics, rhetoric; now, since politics uses the rest of the sciences, and since, again, it legislates as to what we are to do and what we are to abstain from, the end of this science must include those of the others, so that this end must be the good for man. For even if the end is the same for a single man and for a state, that of the state seems at all events something greater and more complete whether to attain or to preserve; though it is worth while to attain the end merely for one man, it is finer and more godlike to attain it for a nation or for city-states. These, then, are the ends at which our inquiry aims, since it is political science, in one sense of that term.

Our discussion will be adequate if it has as much clearness as the subject-matter admits of, for precision is not to be sought for alike in all discussions, any more than in all the products of the crafts. Now fine and just actions, which political science investigates, admit of much variety and fluctuation of opinion, so that they may be thought to exist only by convention, and not by nature. And goods also give rise to a similar fluctuation because they bring harm to many people; for before now men have been undone by reason of their wealth, and others by reason of their courage. We must be content, then, in speaking of such subjects and with such premises to indicate the truth roughly and in outline, and in speaking about things which are only for the most part true and with premises of the same kind to reach conclusions that are no better. In the same spirit, therefore, should each type of statement be *received;* for it is the mark of an educated man to look for precision in each class of things just so far as the nature of the subject admits; it is evidently equally foolish to accept probable reasoning from a mathematician and to demand from a rhetorician scientific proofs.

Now each man judges well the things he knows, and of these he is a good judge. And so the man who has been educated in a subject is a good judge of that subject, and the man who has received an all-around education is a good judge in general. Hence a young man is not a proper hearer of lectures on political science; for he is inexperienced in the actions that occur in life, but its discussions start from these and are about these; and, further, since he tends to follow his passions, his study will be vain and unprofitable because the end aimed at is not knowledge but action. And it makes no difference whether he is young in years or youthful in character; the defect does not depend on time, but on his living, and pursuing each successive object, as passion directs. For to such persons, as to the incontinent, knowledge brings no profit; but to those who desire and act in accordance with a rational principle knowledge about such matters will be of great benefit.

These remarks about the student, the sort of treatment to be expected, and the purpose of the inquiry, may be taken as our preface.

Let us resume our inquiry and state, in view of the fact that all knowledge and every pursuit aims at some good, what it is that we say political science aims at and what is the highest of all goods achievable by action. Verbally there is very general agreement; for both the general run of men and people of superior refinement say that it is happiness, and identify living well and doing well with being happy; but with regard to what happiness is they differ, and the many do not give the same account as the wise. For the former think it is some plain and obvious thing, like pleasure, wealth, or honour; they differ, however, from one another—and often even the same man identifies it with different things, with health when he is ill, with wealth when he is poor; but, conscious of their ignorance, they admire those who proclaim some great ideal that is above their comprehension. Now some thought that apart from these many goods there is another which is self-subsistent and causes the goodness of all these as well. To examine all the opinions that have been held were perhaps somewhat fruitless; enough to examine those that are most prevalent or that seem to be arguable.

Let us not fail to notice, however, that there is a difference between arguments from and those to the first principles. For Plato, too, was right in raising this question and asking, as he used to do, 'are we on the way from or to the first principles?' There is a difference, as there is in a race-course between the course from the judges to the turning-point and the way back. For, while we must begin with what is known, things are objects of knowledge in two senses—some to us, some without qualification. Presumably, then, *we* must begin with things known to *us*. Hence any one who is to listen intelligently to lectures about what is noble and just and, generally, about the subjects of political science must have been brought up in good habits. For the fact is the starting-point, and if this is sufficiently plain to him, he will not at the start need the reason as well; and the man who has been well brought up has or can easily get starting-points. And as for him who neither has nor can get them, let him hear the words of Hesiod:

> Far best is he who knows all things himself;
> Good, he that hearkens when men counsel right;
> But he who neither knows, nor lays to heart
> Another's wisdom, is a useless wight.

Let us, however, resume our discussion from the point at which we digressed. To judge from the lives that men lead, most men, and men of the most vulgar type, seem (not without some ground) to identify the good, or happiness, with pleasure; which is the reason why they love the life of enjoyment. For there are, we may say, three prominent types of life—that just mentioned, the political, and thirdly the contemplative life. Now the mass of mankind are evidently quite slavish in their tastes, preferring a life suitable to beasts, but they get some ground for their view from the fact that many of those in high places share the tastes of Sardanapalus. A consideration of the prominent types of life shows that people of superior refinement and of active disposition identify happiness with honour; for this is, roughly speaking, the end of the political life. But it seems too superficial to be what we are looking for, since it is thought to depend on those who bestow honour rather than on him who receives it, but the good we divine to be something proper to a man and not easily taken from him. Further, men seem to pursue honour in order that they may be assured of their goodness; at least it is by men of practical wisdom that they seek to be honoured, and among those who know them, and on the ground of their virtue; clearly, then, according to them, at any rate, virtue is better. And perhaps one might even suppose this to be, rather than honour, the end of the political life. But even this appears somewhat incomplete; for possession of virtue seems actually compatible with being asleep, or with lifelong inactivity, and, further, with the greatest sufferings and misfortunes; but a man who was living so no one would call happy, unless he were maintaining a thesis at all costs. But enough of this; for the subject has been sufficiently treated even in the current discussions. Third comes the contemplative life, which we shall consider later.

The life of money-making is one undertaken under compulsion, and wealth is evidently not the good we are seeking; for it is merely useful and for the sake of something else. And so one might rather take the aforenamed objects to be ends; for they are loved for themselves. But it is evident that not even these are ends; yet many arguments have been thrown away in support of them. Let us leave this subject, then.

Let us again return to the good we are seeking, and ask what it can be. It seems different in different actions and arts; it is different in medicine, in strategy, and in other arts likewise. What then is the good of each? Surely that for whose sake everything else is done. In medicine this is health, in strategy victory, in architecture a house, in any other sphere something else, and in every action and pursuit the end; for it is for the sake of this that all men do whatever else they do. Therefore, if there is an end for all that we do, this will be the good achievable by action, and if there are more than one, these will be the goods achievable by action.

So the argument has by a different course reached the same point; but we must try to state this even more clearly. Since there are evidently more than one end, and we choose some of these (e.g. wealth, flutes, and in general instruments) for the sake of something else, clearly not all ends are final ends; but the chief good is evidently something final. Therefore, if there is only one final end, this will be what we are seeking, and if there are more than one, the most final of these will be what we are seeking. Now we call that which is in itself worthy of pursuit more final than that which is worthy of pursuit for the sake of something else, and that which is never desirable for the sake of something else more final than the things that are desirable both in themselves and for the sake of that other thing, and therefore we call final without qualification that which is always desirable in itself and never for the sake of something else.

Now such a thing happiness, above all else, is held to be; for this we choose always for itself and never for the sake of something else, but honour, pleasure, reason, and every virtue we choose indeed for themselves (for if nothing resulted from them we should still choose each of them), but we choose them also for the sake of happiness, judging that by means of them we shall be happy. Happiness, on the other hand, no one chooses for the sake of these, nor in general, for anything other than itself.

From the point of view of self-sufficiency the same result seems to follow; for the final good is thought to be self-sufficient. Now by self-sufficient we do not mean that which is sufficient for a man by himself, for one who lives a solitary life, but also for parents, children, wife, and in general for his friends and fellow citizens, since man is born for citizenship. But some limit must be set to this; for if we extend our requirements to ancestors and descendants and friends' friends we are in for an infinite series. Let us examine this question, however, on another occasion; the self-sufficient we now define as that which when isolated makes life desirable and lacking in nothing; and such we think happiness to be; and further we think it most desirable of all things, without being counted as one good thing among others—if it were so counted it would clearly be made more desirable by the addition of even the least of goods; for that which is added becomes an excess of goods, and of goods the greater is always more desirable. Happiness, then, is something final and self-sufficient, and is the end of action.

Presumably, however, to say that happiness is the chief good seems a platitude, and a clearer account of what it is is still desired. This might perhaps be given, if we could first ascertain the function of man. For just as for a flute-player, a sculptor, or any artist, and, in general, for all things that have a function or activity, the good and the 'well' is thought to reside in the function, so would it seem to be for man, if he has a function. Have the carpenter, then, and the tanner certain functions or activities, and has man none? Is he born without a function? Or as eye, hand, foot, and in general each of the parts evidently has a function, may one lay it down that man similarly has a function apart from all these? What then can this be? Life seems to be common even to plants, but we are seeking what is peculiar to man. Let us exclude, therefore, the life of nutrition and growth. Next there would be a life of perception, but *it* also seems to be common even to the horse, the ox, and every animal. There remains, then, an active life of the element that has a rational principle; of this, one part has such a principle in the sense of being obedient to one, the other in the sense of possessing one and exercising thought. And, as 'life of the rational element' also has two meanings, we must state that life in the sense of activity is what we mean; for this seems to be the more proper sense of the term. Now if the function of man is an activity of soul which follows or implies a rational principle, and if we say 'a so-and-so' and 'a good so-and-so' have a function which is the same in kind, e.g. a lyre-player and a good lyre-player, and so without qualification in all cases, eminence in respect of goodness being added to the name of the function (for the function of a lyre-player is to play the lyre, and that of a good lyre-player is to do so well): if this is the case, [and we state the function of man to be a certain kind of life, and this to be an activity or actions of the soul implying a rational principle, and the function of a good man to be the good and noble performance of these, and if any action is well performed when it is performed in accordance with the appropriate excellence: if this is the case,] human good turns out to be activity of soul in accordance with virtue, and if there are more than one virtue, in accordance with the best and most complete.

But we must add 'in a complete life'. For one swallow does not make a summer, nor does one day; and so too one day, or a short time, does not make a man blessed and happy.

Let this serve as an outline of the good; for we must presumably first sketch it roughly, and then later fill in the details. But it would seem that any one is capable of carrying on and articulating what has once been well outlined, and that time is a good discoverer or partner in such a work; to which facts the advances of the arts are due; for any one can add what is lacking. And we must also remember what has been said before, and not look for precision in all things alike, but in each class of things such precision as accords with the subject-matter, and so much as is appropriate to the inquiry. For a carpenter and a geometer investigate the right angle in different ways; the former does so in so far as the right angle is useful for his work, while the latter inquires what it is or what sort of thing it is; for he is a spectator of the truth. We must act in the same way, then, in all other matters as well, that our main task may not be subordinated to minor questions. Nor must we demand the cause in all matters alike; it is enough in some cases that the *fact* be well established, as in the case of the first principles; the fact is the primary thing or first principle. Now of first principles we see some by induction, some by perception, some by a certain habituation, and others too in other ways. But each set of principles we must try to investigate in the natural way, and we must take pains to state them definitely, since they have a great influence on what follows. For the beginning is thought to be more than half of the whole, and many of the questions we ask are cleared up by it.

We must consider it, however, in the light not only of our conclusion and our premisses, but also of what is commonly said about it; for with a true view all the data harmonize, but with a false one the facts soon clash. Now goods have been divided into three classes, and some are described as external, others as relating to soul or to body; we call those that relate to soul most properly and truly goods, and physical actions and activities we class as relating to soul. Therefore our account must be sound, at least according to this view, which is an old one and agreed on by philosophers. It is correct also in that we identify the end with certain actions and activities; for thus it falls among goods of the soul and not among external goods. Another belief which harmonizes with our account is that the happy man lives well and does well; for we have practically defined happiness as a sort of good life and good action. The characteristics that are looked for in happiness seem also, all of them, to belong to what we have defined happiness as being. For some identify happiness with virtue, some with practical wisdom, others with a kind of philosophic wisdom, others with these, or one of these, accompanied by pleasure or not without pleasure; while others include also external prosperity. Now some of these views have been held by many men and men of old, others by a few eminent persons; and it is not probable that either of these should be entirely mistaken, but rather than they should be right in at least some one respect or even in most respects.

With those who identify happiness with virtue or some one virtue our account is in harmony; for to virtue belongs virtuous activity. But it makes, perhaps, no small difference whether we place the chief good in possession or in use, in state of mind or in activity. For the state of mind may exist without producing any good result, as in a man who is asleep or in some other way quite inactive, but the activity cannot; for one who has the activity will of necessity be acting, and acting well. And as in the Olympic Games it is not the most beautiful and the strongest that are crowned but those who compete (for it is some of these that are victorious), so those who act win, and rightly win, the noble and good things in life.

Their life is also in itself pleasant. For pleasure is a state of *soul,* and to each man that which he is said to be a lover of is pleasant; e.g. not only is a horse pleasant to the lover of horses, and a spectacle to the lover of sights, but also in the same way just acts are pleasant to the lover of justice and in general virtuous acts to the lover of virtue. Now for most men their pleasures are in conflict with one another because these are not by nature pleasant, but the lovers of what is noble find pleasant the things that are by nature pleasant; and virtuous actions are such, so that these are pleasant for such men as well as in their own nature. Their life, therefore, has no further need of pleasure as a sort of adventitious charm, but has its pleasure in itself. For, besides what we have said, the man who does not rejoice in noble actions is not even good; since no one would call a man just who did not enjoy acting justly, nor any man liberal who did not enjoy liberal actions; and similarly in all other cases. If this is so, virtuous actions must be in themselves pleasant. But they are also *good* and *noble,* and have each of these attributes in the highest degree, since the good man judges well about their attributes; his judgment is such as we have described. Happiness then is the best, noblest, and most pleasant thing in the world, and these attributes are not severed as in the inscription at Delos—

> Most noble is that which is justest, and best is health;
> But pleasantest is it to win what we love.

For all these properties belong to the best activities; and these, or one—the best—of these, we identify with happiness.

Yet evidently, as we said, it needs the external goods as well; for it is impossible, or not easy, to do noble acts without the proper equipment. In many actions we use friends and riches and political power as instruments; and there are some things the lack of which takes the lustre from happiness, as good birth, goodly children, beauty; for the man who is very ugly in appearance or ill-born or solitary and childless is not very likely to be happy, and perhaps a man would be still less likely if he had thoroughly bad children or friends or had lost good children or friends by death. As we said, then, happiness seems to need this sort of prosperity in addition; for which reason some identify happiness with good fortune, though others identify it with virtue.

For this reason also the question is asked, whether happiness is to be acquired by learning or by habituation or some other sort of training, or comes in virtue of some divine providence or again by chance. Now if there is *any* gift of the gods to men, it is reasonable that happiness should be god-given, and most surely god-given of all human things inasmuch as it is the best. But this question would perhaps be more appropriate to another inquiry; happiness seems, however, even if it is not god-sent but comes as a result of virtue and some process of learning or training, to be among the most god-like things; for that which is the prize and end of virtue seems to be the best thing in the world, and something godlike and blessed.

It will also on this view be very generally shared; for all who are not maimed as regards their potentiality for virtue may win it by a certain kind of study and care. But if it is better to be happy thus than by chance, it is reasonable that the facts should be so, since everything that depends on the action of nature is by nature as good as it can be, and similarly everything that depends on art or any rational cause, and especially if it depends on the best of all causes. To entrust to chance what is greatest and most noble would be a very defective arrangement.

The answer to the question we are asking is plain also from the definition of happiness; for it has been said to be a virtuous activity of soul, of a certain kind. Of the remaining goods, some must necessarily pre-exist as conditions of happiness, and others are naturally co-operative and useful as instruments. And this will be found to agree with what we said at the outset; for we stated the end of political science to be the best end, and political science spends most of its pains on making the citizens to be of a certain character, viz. good and capable of noble acts.

It is natural, then, that we call neither ox nor horse nor any other of the animals happy; for none of them is capable of sharing in such activity. For this reason also a boy is not happy; for he is not yet capable of such acts, owing to his age; and boys who are called happy are being congratulated by reason of the hopes we have for them. For there is required, as we said, not only complete virtue but also a complete life, since many changes occur in life, and all manner of chances, and the most prosperous may fall into great misfortunes in old age, as is told of Priam in the Trojan Cycle; and one who has experienced such chances and has ended wretchedly no one calls happy.

Book II – The Definition of Moral Virtue

Virtue, then, being of two kinds, intellectual and moral, intellectual virtue in the main owes both its birth and its growth to teaching (for which reason it requires experience and time), while moral virtue comes about as a result of habit, whence also its name *ethike* is one that is formed by a slight variation from the word *ethos* (habit). From this it is also plain that none of the moral virtues arises in us by nature; for nothing that exists by nature can form a habit contrary to its nature. For instance the stone which by nature moves downwards cannot be habituated to move upwards, not even if one tries to train it by throwing it up ten thousand times; nor can fire be habituated to move downwards, nor can anything else that by nature behaves in one way be trained to behave in another. Neither by nature, then, nor contrary to nature do the virtues arise in us; rather we are adapted by nature to receive them, and are made perfect by habit.

Again, of all the things that come to us by nature we first acquire the potentiality and later exhibit the activity (this is plain in the case of the senses; for it was not by often seeing or often hearing that we got these senses, but on the contrary we had them before we used them, and did not come to have them by using them); but the virtues we get by first exercising them, as also happens in the case of the arts as well. For the things we have to learn before we can do them, we learn by doing them, e.g. men become builders by building and lyre-players by playing the lyre; so too we become just by doing just acts, temperate by doing temperate acts, brave by doing brave acts.

This is confirmed by what happens in states; for legislators make the citizens good by forming habits in them, and this is the wish of every legislator, and those who do not effect it miss their mark, and it is in this that a good constitution differs from a bad one.

Again, it is from the same causes and by the same means that every virtue is both produced and destroyed, and similarly every art; for it is from playing the lyre that both good and bad lyre-players are produced. And the corresponding statement is true of builders and of all the rest; men will be good or bad builders as a result of building well or badly. For if this were not so, there would have been no need of a teacher, but all men would have been born good or bad at their craft. This, then, is the case with the virtues also; by doing the acts that we do in our transactions with other men we become just or unjust, and by doing the acts that we do in the presence of danger, and being habituated to feel fear or confidence, we become brave or cowardly. The same is true of appetites and feelings of anger; some men become temperate and good-tempered, others self-indulgent and irascible, by behaving in one way or the other in the appropriate circumstances. Thus, in one word, states of character arise out of like activities. This is why the activities we exhibit must be of a certain kind; it is because the states of character correspond to the differences between these. It makes no small difference, then, whether we form habits of one kind or of another from our very youth; it makes a very great difference, or rather *all* the difference.

Since, then, the present inquiry does not aim at theoretical knowledge like the others (for we are inquiring not in order to know what virtue is, but in order to become good, since otherwise our inquiry would have been of no use), we must examine the nature of actions, namely how we ought to do them; for these determine also the nature of the states of character that are produced, as we have said. Now, that we must act according to the right rule is a common principle and must be assumed— it will be discussed later, i.e. both what the right rule is, and how it is related to the other virtues. But this must be agreed upon beforehand, that the whole account of matters of conduct must be given in outline and not precisely, as we said at the very beginning that the accounts we demand must be in accordance with the subject-matter; matters concerned with conduct and questions of what is good for us have no fixity, any more than matters of health. The general account being of this nature, the account of particular cases is yet more lacking in exactness; for they do not fall under any art or precept but the agents themselves must in each case consider what is appropriate to the occasion, as happens also in the art of medicine or of navigation.

But though our present account is of this nature we must give what help we can. First, then, let us consider this, that it is the nature of such things to be destroyed by defect and excess, as we can see in the case of strength and of health (for to gain light on things imperceptible we must use the evidence of sensible things); both excessive and defective exercise destroy the strength, and similarly drink or food which is above or below a certain amount destroys the health, while that which is proportionate both produces and increases and preserves it. So too is it, then, in the case of temperance and courage and the other virtues. For the man who flies from and fears everything and does not stand his ground against anything becomes a coward, and the man who fears nothing at all but goes to meet every danger becomes rash; and similarly the man who indulges in every pleasure and abstains from none becomes self-indulgent, while the man who shuns every pleasure, as boors do, becomes in a way insensible; temperance and courage, then, are destroyed by excess and defect, and preserved by the mean.

But not only are the sources and causes of their origination and growth the same as those of their destruction, but also the sphere of their actualization will be the same; for this is also true of the things which are more evident to sense, e.g. of strength; it is produced by taking much food and undergoing much exertion, and it is the strong man that will be most able to do these things. So too is it with the virtues; by abstaining from pleasures we become temperate, and it is when we have become so that we are most able to abstain from them; and similarly too in the case of courage; for by being habituated to despise things that are terrible and to stand our ground against them we become brave, and it is when we have become so that we shall be most able to stand our ground against them.

We must take as a sign of states of character the pleasure or pain that ensues on acts; for the man who abstains from bodily pleasures and delights in this very fact is temperate, while the man who is annoyed at it is self-indulgent, and he who stands his ground against things that are terrible and delights in this or at least is not pained is brave, while the man who is pained is a coward. For moral excellence is concerned with pleasures and pains; it is on account of the pleasure that we do bad things, and on account of the pain that we abstain from noble ones. Hence we ought to have been brought up in a particular way from our very youth, as Plato says, so as both to delight in and to be pained by the things that we ought; for this is the right education.

Again, if the virtues are concerned with actions and passions, and every passion and every action is accompanied by pleasure and pain, for this reason also virtue will be concerned with pleasures and pains. This is indicated also by the fact that punishment is inflicted by these means; for it is a kind of cure, and it is the nature of cures to be effected by contraries.

Again, as we said but lately, every state of soul has a nature relative to and concerned with the kind of things by which it tends to be made worse or better; but it is by reason of pleasures and pains that men become bad, by pursuing and avoiding these—either the pleasures and pains they ought not or when they ought not or as they ought not, or by going wrong in one of the other similar ways that may be distinguished. Hence men even define the virtues as certain states of impassivity and rest; not well, however, because they speak absolutely, and do not say 'as one ought' and 'as one ought not' and 'when one ought or ought not,' and the other things that may be added. We assume, then, that this kind of excellence tends to do what is best with regard to pleasures and pains, and vice does the contrary.

The following facts also may show us that virtue and vice are concerned with these same things. There being three objects of choice and three of avoidance, the noble, the advantageous, the pleasant, and their contraries, the base, the injurious, the painful, about all of these the good man tends to go right and the bad man to go wrong and especially about pleasure; for this is common to the animals, and also it accompanies all objects of choice; for even the noble and the advantageous appear pleasant.

Again, it has grown up with us all from our infancy; this is why it is difficult to rub off this passion, engrained as it is in our life. And we measure even our actions, some of us more and others less, by the rule of pleasure and pain. For this reason, then, our whole inquiry must be about these; for to feel delight and pain rightly or wrongly has no small effect on our actions.

Again, it is harder to fight with pleasure than with anger, to use Heraclitus' phrase, but both art and virtue are always concerned with what is harder; for even the good is better when it is harder. Therefore for this reason also the whole concern both of virtue and of political science is with pleasures and pains; for the man who uses these well will be good, he who used them badly bad.

That virtue, then, is concerned with pleasures and pains, and that by the acts from which it arises it is both increased and, if they are done differently, destroyed, and that the acts from which it arose are those in which it actualizes itself—let this be taken as said.

The questions might be asked, what we mean by saying that we must become just by doing just acts, and temperate by doing temperate acts; for if men do just and temperate acts, they are already just and temperate, exactly as, if they do what is in accordance with the laws of grammar and music, they are grammarians and musicians.

Or is this not true even of the arts? It is possible to do something that is in accordance with the laws of grammar, either by chance or at the suggestion of another. A man will be a grammarian, then, only when he has both done something grammatical and done it grammatically; and this means doing it in accordance with the grammatical knowledge within himself.

Again, the case of the arts and that of the virtues are not similar; for the products of the arts have their goodness in themselves, so that it is enough that they should have a certain character, but if the acts that are in accordance with the virtues have themselves a certain character it does not follow that they are done justly or temperately. The agent also must be in a certain condition when he does them; in the first place he must have knowledge, secondly he must choose the acts, and choose them for their own sakes, and thirdly his action must proceed from a firm and unchangeable character. These are not reckoned in as conditions of the possession of the arts, except the bare knowledge; but as a condition of the possession of the virtues knowledge has little or no weight, while the other conditions count not for a little but for everything, i.e. the very conditions which result from often doing just and temperate acts.

Actions, then, are called just and temperate when they are such as the just or the temperate man would do; but it is not the man who does these that is just and temperate, but the man who also does them *as* just and temperate men do them. It is well said, then, that it is by doing just acts that the just man is produced, and by doing temperate acts the temperate man; without doing these no one would have even a prospect of becoming good.

But most people do not do these, but take refuge in theory and think they are being philosophers and will become good in this way, behaving somewhat like patients who listen attentively to their doctors, but do none of the things they are ordered to do. As the latter will not be made well in body by such a course of treatment, the former will not be made well in soul by such a course of philosophy.

Next we must consider what virtue is. Since things that are found in the soul are of three kinds—passions, faculties, states of character, virtue must be one of these. By passions I mean appetite, anger, fear, confidence, envy, joy, friendly feeling, hatred, longing, emulation, pity, and in general the feelings that are accompanied by pleasure or pain; by faculties the things in virtue of which we are said to be capable of feeling these, e.g. of becoming angry or being pained or feeling pity; by states of character the things in virtue of which we stand well or badly with reference to the passions, e.g. with reference to anger we stand badly if we feel it violently or too weakly, and well if we feel it moderately; and similarly with reference to the other passions.

Now neither the virtues nor the vices are *passions,* because we are not called good or bad on the ground of our passions, but are so called on the ground of our virtues and our vices, and because we are neither praised nor blamed for our passions (for the man who feels fear or anger is not praised, nor is the man who simply feels anger blamed, but the man who feels it in a certain way), but for our virtues and our vices we *are* praised or blamed.

Again we feel anger and fear without choice, but the virtues are modes of choice or involve choice. Further, in respect of the passions we are said to be moved, but in respect of the virtues and the vices we are said not to be moved but to be disposed in a particular way.

For these reasons also they are not *faculties;* for we are neither called good nor bad, nor praised nor blamed, for the simple capacity of feeling the passions; again, we have the faculties by nature, but we are not made good or bad by nature; we have spoken of this before.

If, then, the virtues are neither passions nor faculties, all that remains is that they should be *states of character.*

Thus we have stated what virtue is in respect of its genus.

We must, however, not only describe virtue as a state of character, but also say what sort of state it is. We may remark, then, that every virtue or excellence both brings into good condition the thing of which it is the excellence and makes the work of that thing be done well; e.g. the excellence of the eye makes both the eye and its work good; for it is by the excellence of the eye that we see well. Similarly the excellence of the horse makes a horse both good in itself and good at running and at carrying its rider and at awaiting the attack of the enemy. Therefore, if this is true in every case, the virtue of man also will be the state of character which makes a man good and which makes him do his own work well.

How this is to happen we have stated already, but it will be made plain also by the following consideration of the specific nature of virtue. In everything that is continuous and divisible it is possible to take more, less, or an equal amount, and that either in terms of the thing itself or relatively to us; and the equal is an intermediate between excess and defect. By the intermediate in the object I mean that which is equidistant from each of the extremes, which is one and the same for all men; by the intermediate relatively to us that which is neither too much nor too little—and this is not one, nor the same for all. For instance, if ten is many and two is few, six is the intermediate, taken in terms of the object; for it exceeds and is exceeded by an equal amount; this is intermediate according to arithmetical proportion. But the intermediate relatively to us is not to be taken so; if ten pounds are too much for a particular person to eat and two too little, it does not follow that the trainer will order six pounds; for this also is perhaps too much for the person who is to take it, or too little—too little for Milo, too much for the beginner in athletic exercises. The same is true of running and wrestling. Thus a master of any art avoids excess and defect, but seeks the intermediate and chooses this—the intermediate not in the object but relatively to us.

If it is thus, then, that every art does its work well—by looking to the intermediate and judging its works by this standard (so that we often say of good works of art that it is not possible either to take away or to add anything, implying that excess and defect destroy the goodness of works of art, while the mean preserves it; and good artists, as we say, look to this in their work), and if, further, virtue is more exact and better than any art, as nature also is, then virtue must have the quality of aiming at the intermediate. I mean moral virtue; for it is this that is concerned with passions and actions, and in these there is excess, defect, and the intermediate. For instance, both fear and confidence and appetite and anger and pity and in general pleasure and pain may be felt both too much and too little, and in both cases not well; but to feel them at the right times, with reference to the right objects, towards the right people, with the right motive, and in the right way, is what is both intermediate and best, and this is characteristic of virtue. Similarly with regard to actions also there is excess, defect, and the intermediate. Now virtue is concerned with passions and actions, in which excess is a form of failure, and so is defect, while the intermediate is praised and is a form of success; and being praised and being successful are both characteristics of virtue. Therefore virtue is a kind of mean, since, as we have seen, it aims at what is intermediate.

Again, it is possible to fail in many ways (for evil belongs to the class of the unlimited, as the Pythagoreans conjectured, and good to that of the limited), while to succeed is possible only in one way (for which reason also one is easy and the other difficult—to miss the mark easy, to hit it difficult); for these reasons also, then, excess and defect are characteristics of vice, and the mean of virtue;

> For men are good in but one way, but bad in many.

Virtue, then, is a state of character concerned with choice, lying in a mean, i.e. the mean relative to us, this being determined by a rational principle, and by that principle by which the man of practical wisdom would determine it. Now it is a mean between two vices, that which depends on excess and that which depends on defect; and again it is a mean because the vices respectively fall short of or exceed what is right in both passions and actions, while virtue both finds and chooses that which is intermediate. Hence in respect of its substance and the definition which states its essence virtue is a mean, with regard to what is best and right an extreme.

But not every action nor every passion admits of a mean; for some have names that already imply badness, e.g. spite, shamelessness, envy, and in the case of actions adultery, theft, murder; for all of these and suchlike things imply by their names that they are themselves bad, and not the excesses or deficiencies of them. It is not possible, then, ever to be right with regard to them; one must always be wrong. Nor does goodness or badness with regard to such things depend on committing adultery with the right woman, at the right time, and in the right way, but simply to do any of them is to go wrong. It would be equally absurd, then, to expect that in unjust, cowardly, and voluptuous action there should be a mean, an excess, and a deficiency; for at that rate there would be a mean of excess and of deficiency, an excess of excess, and a deficiency of deficiency. But as there is no excess and deficiency of temperance and courage because what is intermediate is in a sense an extreme, so too of the actions we have mentioned there is no mean nor any excess and deficiency, but however they are done they are wrong; for in general there is neither a mean of excess and deficiency, nor excess and deficiency of a mean.

EPICURUS

(341-270)

Independence of circumstances we regard as a great good; not because we wish to dispense altogether with external advantages, but in order that, if our possessions are few, we may be content with what we have...

Three schools of thought apart from the philosophical system of Plato and Aristotle emerged during the pre-Christian era in GreeceóSkepticism, Epicureanism, and Stoicism. The latter two are represented here by Epicurus, Epictetus, and Marcus Aurelius.
Epicurus, in a letter to a friend, outlined the fundamental principles of the pursuit of pleasure, a philosophical tradition that had been given earlier expression by Aristippus, one of the many young men inspired by Socrates. In place of the simple view of Aristippus, who put a premium on the attainment of immediate and intense pleasure, Epicurus argued for a more thoughtful approach to life that emphasized tranquility and the avoidance of pain. Epicurus presented his ideas to the people of Athens in the surroundings of his own gardens and welcomed all, including slaves and women, to the discussions and lectures.

LETTER TO A FRIEND

EPICURUS

We must consider that of desires some are natural, others empty; that of the natural some are necessary, others not; and that of the necessary some are necessary for happiness, others for bodily comfort, and others for life itself. A right understanding of these facts enables us to direct all choice and avoidance toward securing the health of the body and tranquility of the soul; this being the final aim of a blessed life. For the aim of all actions is to avoid pain and fear; and when this is once secured for us the tempest of the soul is entirely quelled, since the living animal no longer needs to wander as though in search of something he lacks, hunting for that by which he can fulfill some need of soul or body. We feel a need of pleasure only when we grieve over its absence; when we stop grieving we are in need of pleasure no longer. Pleasure, then, is the beginning and end of the blessed life. For we recognize it as a good which is both primary and kindred to us. From pleasure we begin every act of choice and avoidance; and to pleasure we return again, using the feeling as the standard by which to judge every good.

Now since pleasure is the good that is primary and most natural to us, for that very reason we do not seize all pleasures indiscriminately; on the contrary we often pass over many pleasures, when greater discomfort accrues to us as a result of them. Similarly we not infrequently judge pains better than pleasures, when the long endurance of a pain yields us a greater pleasure in the end. Thus every pleasure because of its natural kinship to us is good, yet not every pleasure is to be chosen; just as every pain also is an evil, yet that does not mean that all pains are necessarily to be shunned. It is by a scale of comparison and by the consideration of advantages and disadvantages that we must form our judgement on these matters. On particular occasions we may have reason to treat the good as bad, and the bad as good.

Independence of circumstances we regard as a great good: not because we wish to dispense altogether with external advantages, but in order that, if our possessions are few, we may be content with what we have, sincerely believing that those enjoy luxury most who depend on it least, and that natural wants are easily satisfied if we are willing to forego superfluities. Plain fare yields as much pleasure as a luxurious table, provided the pain of real want is removed; bread and water can give exquisite delight to hungry and thirsty lips. To form the habit of a simple and modest diet, therefore, is the way to health: it enables us to perform the needful employments of life without shrinking, it puts us in better condition to enjoy luxuries when they are offered, and it renders us fearless of fortune.

Accordingly, when we argue that pleasure is the end and aim of life, we do not mean the pleasure of prodigals and sensualists, as some of our ignorant or prejudiced critics persist in mistaking us. We mean the pleasure of being free from pain of body and anxiety of mind. It is not a continual round of drunken debauches and lecherous delights, nor the enjoyment of fish and other delicacies of a wealthy table, which produce a pleasant life; but sober reasoning, searching out the motives of choice and avoidance, and escaping the bondage of opinion, to which the greatest disturbances of spirit are due.

The first step and the greatest good is prudence—a more precious thing than philosophy even, for all the other virtues are sprung from it. By prudence we learn that we can live pleasurably only if we live prudently, honorably, and justly, while contrariwise to live prudently, honorably, and justly guarantees a life that is pleasurable as well. The virtues are by nature bound up with a pleasant life, and a pleasant life is inseparable from them in turn.

Is there any better and wiser man than he who holds reverent beliefs about the gods, is altogether free from the fear of death, and has serenely contemplated the basic tendencies of natural law? Such a man understands that the limit of good things is easy to attain, and that evils are slight either in duration or in intensity. He laughs at Destiny, which so many accept as all-powerful. Some things, he observes, occur of necessity, others by chance, and still others through our own agency. Necessity is irresponsible, chance is inconstant, but our own actions are free, and it is to them that praise and blame are properly attached. It would be better even to believe the myths about the gods than to submit to the Destiny which the natural philosophers teach. For the old superstitions at least offer some faint hope of placating the gods by worship, but the Necessity of the scientific philosophers is absolutely unyielding. As to chance, the wise man does not deify it as most men do; for if it were divine it would not be without order. Nor will he accept the view that it is a universal cause even though of a wavering kind; for he believes that what chance bestows is not the good and evil that determine a man's blessedness in life, but the starting-points from which each person can arrive at great good or great evil. He esteems the misfortune of the wise above the prosperity of a fool; holding it better that well chosen courses of action should fail than that ill chosen ones should succeed by mere chance.

Meditate on these and like precepts day and night, both privately and with some companion who is of kindred disposition. Thereby shall you never suffer disturbance, waking or asleep, but shall live like a god among men. For a man who lives constantly among immortal blessings is surely more than mortal.

EPICTETUS

(C. 50-138)

"Demand not that events should happen as you wish; but wish them to happen as they do happen, and you will go on well."

While the Epicureans were advancing a hedonistic creed, their great rivals, the Stoics, were denouncing the pursuit of pleasure as ignoble. The world, they insisted, is part of a divine rational order, and human purpose must be the merging of the individual self into harmonious union with that order. Begun in Athens by Zeno, who gave the philosophy its name by conducting his lessons from a stoa (porch), Stoicism became a dominant point of view, surviving the decline of Greece, finding significant adherents in Roman culture, and contributing significantly to the development of Christianity.

In *The Enchiridion* (manual or handbook) Arrian, a student of Epictetus, condensed the master's teachings into a digest of his central doctrines, emphasizing the self-discipline for which Stoicism is so well-known.

THE ENCHIRIDION

EPICTETUS

I

There are things which are within our power, and there are things which are beyond our power. Within our power are opinion, aim, desire, aversion, and, in one word, whatever affairs are our own. Beyond our power are body, property, reputation, office, and, in one word, whatever are not properly our own affairs.

Now the things within our power are by nature free, unrestricted, unhindered; but those beyond our power are weak, dependent, restricted, alien. Remember, then, that if you attribute freedom to things by nature dependent and take what belongs to others for your own, you will be hindered, you will lament, you will be disturbed, you will find fault both with gods and men. But if you take for your own only that which is your own and view what belongs to others just as it really is, then no one will ever compel you, no one will restrict you; you will find fault with no one, you will accuse no one, you will do nothing against your will; no one will hurt you, you will not have an enemy, nor will you suffer any harm.

Aiming, therefore, at such great things, remember that you must not allow yourself any inclination, however slight, toward the attainment of the others; but that you must entirely quit some of them, and for the present postpone the rest. But if you would have these, and possess power and wealth likewise, you may miss the latter in seeking the former; and you will certainly fail of that by which alone happiness and freedom are procured.

Seek at once, therefore, to be able to say to every unpleasing semblance, "You are but a semblance and by no means the real thing." And then examine it by those rules which you have; and first and chiefly by this: whether it concerns the things which are within our own power or those which are not; and if it concerns anything beyond our power, be prepared to say that it is nothing to you.

II

Remember that desire demands the attainment of that of which you are desirous; and aversion demands the avoidance of that to which you are averse; that he who fails of the object of his desires is disappointed; and he who incurs the object of his aversion is wretched. If, then, you shun only those undesirable things which you can control, you will never incur anything which you shun; but if you shun sickness, or death, or poverty, you will run the risk of wretchedness. Removed [the habit of] aversion, then, from all things that are not within our power, and apply it to things undesirable which are within our power. But for the present, altogether restrain desire; for if you desire any of the things not within our own power, you must necessarily be disappointed; and you are not yet secure of those which are within our power, and so are legitimate objects of desire. Where it is practically necessary for you to pursue or avoid anything, do even this with discretion and gentleness and moderation.

III

With regard to whatever objects either delight the mind or contribute to use or are tenderly beloved, remind yourself of what nature they are, beginning with the merest trifles: if you have a favorite cup, that it is but a cup of which you are fond of—for thus, if it is broken, you can bear it; if you embrace your child or your wife, that you embrace a mortal—and thus, if either of them dies, you can bear it.

IV

When you set about any action, remind yourself of what nature the action is. If you are going to bathe, represent to yourself the incidents usual in the bath—some persons pouring out, others pushing in, others scolding, others pilfering. And thus you will more safely go about this action if you say to yourself, "I will now go to bathe and keep my own will in harmony with nature." And so with regard to every other action. For thus, if any impediment arises in bathing, you will be able to say, "It was not only to bathe that I desired, but to keep my will in harmony with nature; and I shall not keep it thus if I am out of humor at things that happen."

V

Men are disturbed not by things, but by the views which they take of things. Thus death is nothing terrible, else it would have appeared so to Socrates. But the terror consists in our notion of death, that it is terrible. When, therefore, we are hindered or disturbed, or grieved, let us never impute it to others, but to ourselves—that is, to our own views. It is the action of an uninstructed person to reproach others for his own misfortunes; of one entering upon instruction, to reproach himself; and one perfectly instructed, to reproach neither others nor himself.

VII

As in a voyage, when the ship is at anchor, if you go on shore to get water, you may amuse yourself with picking up a shellfish or a truffle in your way, but your thoughts ought to be bent toward the ship, and perpetually attentive, lest the captain should call, and then you must leave all these things, that you may not have to be carried on board the vessel, bound like a sheep; thus likewise in life, if, instead of a truffle or shellfish, such a thing as a wife or a child be granted you, there is no objection; but if the captain calls, run to the ship, leave all these things, and never look behind. But if you are old, never go far from the ship, lest you should be missing when called for.

VIII

Demand not that events should happen as you wish; but wish them to happen as they do happen, and you will go on well.

XI

Never say of anything, "I have lost it," but, "I have restored it." Has your child died? It is restored. Has your wife died? She is restored. Has your estate been taken away? That likewise is restored. "But it was a bad man who took it." What is it to you by whose hands he who gave it has demanded it again? While he permits you to possess it, hold it as something not your own, as do travelers at an inn.

XII

If you would improve, lay aside such reasonings as these: "If I neglect my affairs, I shall not have a maintenance; if I do not punish my servant, he will be good for nothing." For it were better to die of hunger, exempt from grief and fear, than to live in affluence with perturbation; and it is better that your servant should be bad than you unhappy.

Begin therefore with little things. Is a little oil spilled or a little wine stolen? Say to yourself, "This is the price paid for peace and tranquility; and nothing is to be had for nothing." And when you call your servant, consider that it is possible he may not come at your call; or, if he does, that he may not do what you wish. But it is not at all desirable for him, and very undesirable for you, that it should be in his power to cause you any disturbance.

XIII

If you would improve, be content to be thought foolish and dull with regard to externals. Do not desire to be thought to know anything; and though you should appear to others to be somebody, distrust yourself. For be assured, it is not easy at once to keep your will in harmony with nature and to secure externals; but while you are absorbed in the one, you must of necessity neglect the other.

XIV

If you wish your children and your wife and your friends to live forever, you are foolish, for you wish things to be in your power which are not so, and what belongs to others to be your own. So likewise, if you wish your servant to be without fault, you are foolish, for you wish vice not to be vice but something else. But if you wish not to be disappointed in your desires, that is in your own power. Exercise, therefore, what is in your power. A man's master is he who is able to confer or remove whatever that man seeks or shuns. Whoever then would be free, let him wish nothing, let him decline nothing, which depends on others; else he must necessarily be a slave.

XV

Remember that you must behave as at a banquet. Is anything brought round to you? Put out your hand and take a moderate share. Does it pass by you? Do not stop it. Is it not yet come? Do not yearn in desire toward it, but wait till it reaches you. So with regard to children, wife, office, riches; and you will some time or other be worthy to feast with the gods. And if you do not so much as take the things which are set before you, but are able even to forego them, then you will not only be worthy to feast with the gods, but to rule with them also. For, by thus doing, Diogenes and Heraclitus, and others like them, deservedly became divine, and were so recognized.

XVIII

When a raven happens to croak unluckily, be not overcome by appearances, but discriminate and say, "Nothing is portended to *me,* either to my paltry body, or property, or reputation, or children, or wife. But to *me* all portents are lucky if I will. For whatever happens, it belongs to me to derive advantage therefrom."

XX

Remember that it is not he who gives abuse or blows, who affronts, but the view we take of these things as insulting. When, therefore, anyone provokes you, be assured that it is your own opinion which provokes you. Try, therefore, in the first place, not to be bewildered by appearances. For if you once gain time and respite, you will more easily command yourself.

XXII

If you have an earnest desire toward philosophy, prepare yourself from the very first to have the multitude laugh and sneer, and say, "He is returned to us a philosopher all at once"; and, "Whence this supercilious look?" Now, for your part, do not have a supercilious look indeed, but keep steadily to those things which appear best to you, as one appointed by God to this particular station. For remember that, if you are persistent, those very persons who at first ridiculed will afterwards admire you. But if you are conquered by them, you will incur a double ridicule.

XXIII

If you ever happen to turn your attention to externals, for the pleasure of anyone, be assured that you have ruined your scheme of life. Be content, then, in everything, with being a philosopher; and if you wish to seem so likewise to anyone, appear so to yourself, and it will suffice you.

XXIV

Let not such considerations as these distress you: "I shall live in discredit and be nobody anywhere." For if discredit be an evil, you can no more be involved in evil through another than in baseness. Is it any business of yours, then, to get power or to be admitted to an entertainment? By no means. How than, after all, is this discredit? And how it is true that you will be nobody anywhere when you ought to be somebody in those things only which are within your own power, in which you may be of the greatest consequence? "But my friends will be unassisted." What do you mean by "unassisted"? They will not have money from you, nor will you make them Roman citizens. Who told you, then, that these are among the things within our power, and not rather the affairs of others? And who can give to another the things which he himself has not? "Well, but get them, then, that we too may have a share." If I can get them with the preservation of my own honor and fidelity and self-respect, show me the way and I will get them; but if you require me to lose my own proper good, that you may gain what is no good, consider how unreasonable and foolish you are. Besides, which would you rather have, a sum of money or a faithful and honorable friend? Rather assist me, then, to gain this character than require me to do those things by which I may lose it. Well, but my country, say you, as far as depends upon me, will be unassisted. Here, again, what assistance is this you mean? It will not have porticos nor baths of your providing? And what signifies that? Why, neither does a smith provide it with shoes, nor a shoemaker with arms. It is enough if everyone fully performs his own proper business. And were you to supply it with another faithful and honorable citizen, would not he be of use to it? Yes. Therefore neither are you yourself useless to it. "What place, then," say you, "shall I hold in the state?" Whatever you can hold with the preservation of your fidelity and honor. But if, by desiring to be useful to that, you lose these, how can you serve your country when you have become faithless and shameless?

XXV

Is anyone preferred before you at an entertainment, or in courtesies, or in confidential intercourse? If these things are good, you ought to rejoice that he has them; and if they are evil, do not be grieved that you have them not. And remember that you cannot be permitted to rival others in externals without using the same means to obtain them. For how can he who will not haunt the door of any man, will not attend him, will not praise him, have an equal share with him who does these things? You are unjust, then, and unreasonable if you are unwilling to pay the price for which these things are sold, and would have them for nothing. For how much are lettuces sold? An obulus, for instance. If another, then, paying an obulus, takes the lettuces, and you, not paying it, go without them, do not imagine that he has gained any advantage over you. For as he has the lettuces, so you have the obulus which you did not give. So, in the present case, you have not been invited to such a person's entertainment because you have not paid him the price for which a supper is sold. It is sold for praise; it is sold for attendance. Give him, then, the value if it be for your advantage. But if you would at the same time not pay the one, and yet receive the other, you are unreasonable and foolish. Have you nothing, then, in place of the supper? Yes, indeed, you have—not to praise him whom you do not like to praise; not to bear the insolence of his lackeys.

XXVI

The will of nature may be learned from things upon which we are all agreed. As when our neighbor's boy has broken a cup, or the like, we are ready at once to say, "These are casualties that will happen"; be assured, then, that when your own cup is likewise broken, you ought to be affected just as when another's cup was broken. Now apply this to greater things. Is the child or wife of another dead? There is no one who would not say, "This is an accident of mortality." But if anyone's own child happens to die, it is immediately, "Alas! how wretched am I!" It should be always remembered how we are affected on hearing the same thing concerning others.

XXVII

As a mark is not set up for the sake of missing the aim, so neither does the nature of evil exist in the world.

XXVIII

If a person had delivered up your body to some passer-by, you would certainly be angry. And do you feel no shame in delivering up your own mind to any reviler, to be disconcerted and confounded?

XXIX

In every affair consider what precedes and what follows, and then undertake it. Otherwise you will begin with spirit, indeed, careless of the consequences, and when these are developed, you will shamefully desist. "I would conquer at the Olympic Games." But consider what precedes and what follows, and then, if it be for your advantage, engage in the affair. You must conform to rules, submit to a diet, refrain from dainties; exercise your body, whether you choose it or not, at a stated hour, in heat and cold; you must drink no cold water, and sometimes no wine—in a word, you must give yourself up to your trainer as to a physician. Then, in the combat, you may be thrown into a ditch, dislocate your arm, turn your ankle, swallow an abundance of dust, receive stripes [for negligence], and, after all, lose the victory. When you have reckoned up all this, if your inclination still holds, set about the combat. Otherwise, take notice, you will behave like children who sometimes play wrestlers, sometimes gladiators, sometimes blow a trumpet, and sometimes act a tragedy, when they happen to have seen and admired these shows. Thus you too will be at one time a wrestler, and another a gladiator; now a philosopher, now an orator; but nothing in earnest. Like an ape you mimic all you see, and one thing after another is sure to please you, but is out of favor as soon as it becomes familiar. For you have never entered upon anything considerately: nor after having surveyed and tested the whole matter, but carelessly, and with a halfway zeal. Thus some, when they have seen a philosopher and heard a man speaking like Euphrates—though, indeed, who can speak like him?—have a mind to be philosophers, too. Consider first, man, what the matter is, and what your own nature is able to bear. If you would be a wrestler, consider your shoulders, your back, your thighs: for different persons are made for different things. Do you think that you can act as you do and be a philosopher, that you can eat, drink, be angry, be discontented, as you are now? You must watch, you must labor, you must get the better of certain appetites, must quit your acquaintances, be despised by your servant, be laughed at by those you meet; come off worse than others in everything—in offices, in honors, before tribunals. When you have fully considered all these things, approach, if you please—that is, if, by parting with them, you have a mind to purchase serenity, freedom, and tranquility. If not, do not come hither: do not, like children, be now a philosopher, than a publican, then an orator, and then one of Caesar's officers. These things are not consistent. You must be one man, either good or bad. You must cultivate either your own reason or else externals; apply yourself either to things within or without you—that is, be either a philosopher or one of the mob.

XXXIV

If you are dazzled by the semblance of any promised pleasure, guard yourself against being bewildered by it; but let the affair wait your leisure, and procure yourself some delay. Then bring to your mind both points of time—that in which you shall enjoy the pleasure, and that in which you will repent and reproach yourself, after you have enjoyed it—and set before you, in opposition to these, how you will rejoice and applaud yourself if you abstain. And even though it should appear to you a seasonable gratification, take heed that its enticements and allurements and seductions may not subdue you, but set in opposition to this how much better it is to be conscious of having gained so great a victory.

XXXV

When you do anything from a clear judgment that it ought to be done, never shrink from being seen to do it, even though the world should misunderstand it; for if you are not acting rightly, shun the action itself; if you are, why fear those who wrongly censure you?

XXXVIII

As in walking you take care not to tread upon a nail, or turn your foot, so likewise take care not to hurt the ruling faculty of your mind.

And if we were to guard against this in every action, we should enter upon action more safely.

XXXIX

The body is to everyone the proper measure of its possessions, as the foot is of the shoe. If, therefore, you stop at this, you will keep the measure; but if you move beyond it, you must necessarily be carried forward, as down a precipice; as in the case of a shoe, if you go beyond its fitness to the foot, it comes first to be gilded, then purple, and then studded with jewels. For to that which once exceeds the fit measure there is no bound.

XL

Women from fourteen years old are flattered by men with the title of mistresses. Therefore, perceiving that they are regarded only as qualified to give men pleasure, they begin to adorn themselves, and in that to place all their hopes. It is worth while, therefore, to try that they may perceive themselves honored only so far as they appear beautiful in their demeanor and modestly virtuous.

XLI

It is a mark of want of intellect to spend much time in things relating to the body, as to be immoderate in exercises, in eating and drinking, and in the discharge of other animal functions. These things should be done incidentally and our main strength be applied to our reason.

XLII

When any person does ill by you, or speaks ill of you, remember that he acts or speaks from an impression that it is right for him to do so. Now it is not possible that he should follow what appears right to you, but only what appears so to himself. Therefore, if he judges from false appearances, he is the person hurt, since he, too, is the person deceived. For if anyone takes a true proposition to be false, the proposition is not hurt, but only the man is deceived. Setting out, then, from these principles, you will meekly bear with a person who reviles you, for you will say upon every occasion, "It seemed so to him."

XLIV

These reasonings have no logical connection: "I am richer than you, therefore I am your superior." "I am more eloquent than you, therefore I am your superior." The true logical connection is rather this: "I am richer than you, therefore my possessions must exceed yours." "I am more eloquent than you, therefore my style must surpass yours." But you, after all, consist neither in property nor in style.

XLVI

Never proclaim yourself a philosopher, nor make much talk among the ignorant about your principles, but show them by actions. Thus, at an entertainment, do not discourse how people ought to eat, but eat as you ought. For remember that thus Socrates also universally avoided all ostentation. And when persons came to him and desired to be introduced by him to philosophers, he took them and introduced them; so well did he bear being overlooked. So if ever there should be among the ignorant any discussion of principles, be for the most part silent. For there is great danger in hastily throwing out what is undigested. And if anyone tells you that you know nothing, and you are not nettled at it, then you may be sure that you have really entered on your work. For sheep do not hastily throw up the grass to show the shepherds how much they have eaten, but, inwardly digesting their food, they produce it outwardly in wool and milk. Thus, therefore, do not make an exhibition before the ignorant of your principles, but of the actions to which their digestion gives rise.

XLVIII

The condition and characteristic of a vulgar person is that he never looks for either help or harm from himself, but only from externals. The condition and characteristic of a philosopher is that he looks to himself for all help or harm. The marks of a proficient are that he censures no one, praises no one, blames no one, accuses no one; says nothing concerning himself as being anybody or knowing anything. When he is in any instance hindered or restrained, he accuses himself; and if he is praised, he smiles to himself at the person who praises him; and if he is censured, he makes no defense. But he goes about with the caution of a convalescent, careful of interference with anything that is doing well but not yet quite secure. He restrains desire; he transfers his aversion to those things only which thwart the proper use of our own will; he employs his energies moderately in all directions; if he appears stupid or ignorant, he does not care; and, in a word, he keeps watch over himself as over an enemy and one in ambush.

XLIX

When anyone shows himself vain on being able to understand and interpret the works of Chrysippus, say to yourself: "Unless Chrysippus had written obscurely, this person would have had nothing to be vain of. But what do I desire? To understand nature, and follow her. I ask, then, who interprets her; and hearing that Chrysippus does, I have recourse to him. I do not understand his writings. I seek, therefore, one to interpret *them*." So far there is nothing to value myself upon. And when I find an interpreter, what remains is to make use of his instructions. This alone is the valuable thing. But if I admire merely the interpretation, what do I become more than a grammarian, instead of a philosopher, except, indeed, that instead of Homer I interpret Chrysippus? When anyone, therefore, desires me to read Chrysippus to him, I rather blush when I cannot exhibit actions that are harmonious and consonant with his discourse.

L

Whatever rules you have adopted, abide by them as laws, and as if you would be impious to transgress them; and do not regard what anyone says of you, for this, after all, is no concern of yours. How long, then, will you delay to demand of yourself the noblest improvements, and in no instance to transgress the judgments of reason? You have received the philosophic principles with which you ought to be conversant; and you have been conversant with them. For what other master, then, do you wait as an excuse for this delay in self-reformation? You are no longer a boy but a grown man. If, therefore, you will be negligent and slothful, and always add procrastination to procrastination, purpose to purpose, and fix day after day in which you will attend to yourself, you will insensibly continue to accomplish nothing and, living and dying, remain vulgar of mind. This instant, then, think yourself worthy of living as a man grown up and a proficient. Let whatever appears to be the best be to you an inviolable law. And if any instance of pain or pleasure, glory or disgrace, be set before you, remember that now is the combat, now the Olympiad comes on, nor can it be put off; and that by one failure and defeat honor may be lost or—won. Thus Socrates became perfect, improving himself by everything, following reason alone. And though you are not yet a Socrates, you ought, however, to live as one seeking to be a Socrates.

LI

The first and most necessary topic in philosophy is the practical application of principles, as, *We ought not to lie;* the second is that of demonstration as, *Why it is that we ought not to lie;* the third, that which gives strength and logical connection to the other two, as, *Why this is a demonstration.* For what is demonstration? What is a consequence? What a contradiction? What truth? What falsehood? The third point is then necessary on account of the second; and the second on account of the first. But the most necessary, and that whereon we ought to rest, is the first. But we do just the contrary. For we spend all our time on the third point and employ all our diligence about that, and entirely neglect the first. Therefore, at the same time that we lie, we are very ready to show how it is demonstrated that lying is wrong.

Upon all occasions we ought to have these maxims ready at hand:

> Conduct me, Zeus, and thou, O Destiny,
> Wherever your decrees have fixed my lot.
> I follow cheerfully; and, did I not,
> Wicked and wretched, I must follow still.
>
> Who'er yields properly to Fate is deemed
> Wise among men, and knows the laws of Heaven.

And this third:

> "O Crito, if it thus pleases the gods, thus let it be."
> "Anytus and Melitus may kill me indeed; but hurt me they cannot."

MARCUS AURELIUS

(121-180)

"Whatever is agreeable to you, O universe, is so to me, too."

Marcus Aurelius, Roman Emperor and Stoic, was born in Rome. He came from an aristocratic background and as a small child came to the attention of the Emperor Hadrian. Hadrian arranged for Marcus to receive a structured education in literature, the arts, and philosophy. Eventually, Aurelius became fascinated by the study of philosophy. He was to make this his life long interest. In 138 Hadrian formally adopted Aurelius. In 161 Marcus became Emperor along with his brother Lucius Aurelius Verus. Upon Verus's death in 169 Marcus Aurelius ruled alone.

Marcus Aurelius wrote his great work, *Meditations,* during his reign as Roman Emperor. *Meditations* essentially consists of a series of personal reflections by Aurelius. His reflections constitute a splendid description of the Stoic philosophy. He stresses in his Stoicism that freedom is obtained by detaching one's self from that which cannot be changed. Divine providence must be submitted to.

Marcus Aurelius's writings reveal an Emperor under great pressure. Political rivalries, Christian rebels, and other concerns of state, all seem to have depressed Aurelius. His advocacy of Stoicism was a way for Aurelius to handle the pressures of state. Many continue to find personal solace in his writings.

MEDITATIONS

MARCUS AELIUS AURELIUS ANTONINUS

I-The Cultivation of a Philosophical Mind

The example of my grandfather Verus taught me to be candid and to control my temper. By the memory of my father's character I learnt to be modest and manly. My mother taught me regard for religion, to be generous and open-handed, and neither to do an ill turn to anyone nor even to think of it. She bred me also to a plain and inexpensive way of living.

I owe it to my grandfather that I had not a public education, but had good masters at home. From my tutor I learnt not to identify myself with popular sporting interests, but to work hard, endure fatigue, and not to meddle with other people's affairs. Diognetus taught me to bear freedom and plain dealing in others, and gave me a taste for philosophy. Rusticus first set me to improve my character, and prevented me from running after the vanity of the Sophists.

Apollonius showed me how to give my mind its due freedom, to disregard everything that was not true and reasonable and to maintain an equable temper under the most trying circumstances. Sextus taught me good humour, to be obliging and to bear with the ignorant and thoughtless. From Maximus I learnt to command myself and to put through business efficiently, without drudging or complaint.

From my adoptive father I learnt a smooth and inoffensive temper and a greatness proof against vanity and the impressions of pomp and power; I learnt that it was the part of a prince to check flattery, to have his exchequer well furnished, to be frugal in his expenses, not to worship the gods to superstition, but to be reserved, vigilant and well poised.

I thank the gods that my grandfathers, parents, sister, preceptors, relatives, friends and domestics were almost all persons of probity and that I never happened to disoblige any of them. By the goodness of the gods I was not provoked to expose my infirmities. I owe it to them also that my wife is so deferential, affectionate and frugal; and that when I had a mind to look into philosophy I did not spend too much time in reading or logic-chopping. All these points could never have been guarded without a protection from above.

II-Philosophy, the Mind's Greatest Solace

Put yourself in mind, every morning, that before that night you will meet with some meddlesome, ungrateful and abusive fellow, with some envious or unsociable churl. Remember that their perversity proceeds from ignorance of good and evil; and that since it has fallen to my share to understand the natural beauty of a good action and the deformity of an ill one; since I am satisfied that the disobliging person is of kin to me, our minds being both extracted from the Deity; since no man can do me a real injury because no man can force me to misbehave myself; I cannot therefore hate or be angry with one of my own nature and family. For we are all made for mutual assistance, no less than the parts of the body are for the service of the whole; whence it follows that clashing and opposition are utterly unnatural.

This being of mine consists of body, breath and that part which governs. Put away your books and face the matter itself. As for your body, value it no more than if you were just expiring; it is nothing but a little blood and bones. Your breath is but a little air pumped in and out. But the third part is your mind. Here make a stand. Consider that you are an old man, and do not let this noble part of you languish in slavery any longer. Let it not be overborne with selfish passions; let it not quarrel with fate, or be uneasy at the present, or afraid of the future. Providence shines clearly through the work of the gods. Let these reflections satisfy you, and make them your rule to live by. As for books, cease to be eager for them, that you may die in good humour heartily thanking the gods for what you have had.

Remember that you are a man and a Roman, and let your actions be done with dignity, gravity, humanity, freedom and justice; let every action be done as though it were your last. Have neither insincerity nor self-love. Man has to gain but few points in order to live a happy and godlike life.

And what, after all, is there to be afraid of in death? If the gods exist, you can suffer no harm; and if they do not exist, or take no care of us mortals, a world without gods or providence is not worth a man's while to live in. But the being of the gods, and their concern in human affairs, is beyond dispute; and they have put it in every man's power not to fall into any calamity properly so called.

Living and dying, honour and infamy, pleasure and pain, riches and poverty—all these are common to the virtuous and the depraved, and are therefore intrinsically neither good nor evil. We live but for a moment; our being is in a perpetual flux, our faculties are dim, our bodies tend ever to corruption; the soul is an eddy, fortune is not to be guessed at and posthumous fame is oblivion. To what, then, may we trust? Why, to nothing but philosophy. This is, to keep the interior divinity from injury and disgrace, and superior to pleasure and pain, without any dissembling and pretence, and to acquiesce in one's appointed lot.

III-Of Resoluteness for that which is Best

Observe that the least things and effects in nature are not without charm and beauty, as the little cracks in the crust of a loaf, though not intended by the baker, are agreeable and invite the appetite. Thus figs, when they are ripest, open and gape; and olives, when they are near decaying, are peculiarly attractive. The bending of an ear of corn, the frown of a lion, the foam of a boar, and many other like things, if you take them singly, are far from beautiful; but seen in their natural relations are characteristic and effective. So if a man have but inclination and thought to examine the product of the universe, he will find that the most unpromising appearances have their own appropriate charm.

Do not spend your thoughts upon other people, nor pry into the talk, fancies and projects of another, nor guess at what he is about, or why he is doing it. Think upon nothing but what you could willingly tell about, so that if your soul were laid open there would appear nothing but what was sincere, good-natured and public-spirited. A man thus qualified is a sort of priest and minister of the gods, and makes a right use of the divinity within him. Be cheerful; depend not at all on foreign supports, nor beg your happiness of another; do not throw away your legs to stand upon crutches.

If, in the whole compass of human life, you find anything preferable to justice and truth, temperance and fortitude, or to a mind self-satisfied with its own rational conduct and entirely resigned to fate, then turn to it as to your supreme happiness. But if there be nothing more valuable than the divinity within you, if all things are trifles in comparison with this, then do not divide your allegiance. Let your choice run all one way, and be resolute for that which is best. As for other speculations, throw them once for all out of your head.

IV-Of Loyalty to the Principles of Wisdom

It is the custom of people to go to unfrequented places and to the seashore and to the hills for retirement; and you yourself have often desired this solitude. But, after all, this is only a vulgar fancy, for it is in your power to withdraw into yourself whenever you have a mind to it. One's own heart is a place the most free from crowd and noise in the world if only one's thoughts are serene and the mind well ordered. Make, therefore, frequent use of this retirement, therein to refresh your virtue. And to this end be always provided with a few short, uncontested notions, to keep your understanding true. Do not forget to retire to this solitude of yours; let there be no straining or struggling in the matter, but move at ease.

If understanding be common to us all, then reason, its cause, must be common, too. And so also must the reason which governs conduct by commands and prohibitions be common to us all. Mankind is therefore under one common law and so are fellow-citizens; and the whole world is but one commonwealth, for there is no other society in which mankind can be incorporated.

Do not suppose that you are hurt, and your complaint will cease.

If a man affronts you, do not defer to his opinion, or think just as he would have you do. No; look upon things as reality presents them. When incense is thrown upon the altar, one grain usually falls before another; but it matters not.

Adhere to the principles of wisdom, and those who now take you for a monkey or a beast will make a god of you in a week.

A thing is neither better nor worse for being praised. Do virtues stand in need of a good word, or are they the worse for a bad one? An emerald will shine none the less though its worth be not spoken of.

Whatever is agreeable to You, O Universe, is so to me, too. Your operations are never mis-timed. Whatever Your seasons bring is fruit for me, O Nature. From You all things proceed, subsist in You, and return to You. The poet said, 'Dear City of Cecrops'; shall we not say, 'Dear City of God'?

The greater part of what we say and do is unnecessary; and if this were only retrenched we should have more leisure and less disturbance. This applies to our thoughts also, for impertinence of thought leads to unnecessary action.

Mankind are poor, transitory things; one day in life, and the next turned to ashes. Therefore manage this minute wisely and part with it cheerfully; and like a ripe fruit, when you drop, make your acknowledgments to the tree that bore you.

V-Of Sincerity in Actions

When you feel unwilling to rise early in the morning, make this short speech to yourself: 'I am getting up now to do the business of a man; and am I out of humour for going about that I was made for, and for the sake of which I was sent into the world? Was I then designed for nothing but to doze beneath the counterpane?' Surely action is the end of your being. Look upon the plants and birds, the ants, spiders and bees, and you will see that they are all exerting their nature and busy in their station. Shall not a man act like a man?

Be not ashamed of any action which is in accordance with nature, and never be misled by the fear of censure or reproach. Where honesty prompts you to say or do anything, let not the opinion of others hold you back. Go straight forward, pursuing your own and the common interest.

Some men, when they do you a kindness, ask for the payment of gratitude; others, more modest, remember the favour and look upon you as their debtor. But there are yet other benefactors who forget their good deeds; and these are like the vine, which is satisfied by being fruitful in its kind and bears a bunch of grapes without expecting any thanks for it. A truly kind man never talks of a good turn that he has done, but does another as soon as he can, just like a vine that bears again the next season.

We commonly say that Aesculapius has prescribed riding for one patient, walking for another, a cold bath for a third. In the same way we may say that the nature of the universe has ordered this or that person a disease, loss of limbs or estate, or some such other calamity. For as, in the first case, the word 'prescribed' means a direction for the health of the patient, so, in the latter, it means an application suitable for his constitution and destiny.

Be not uneasy, discouraged or out of humour, because practice falls short of precept in some particulars. If you happen to be vanquished, come on again, and be glad if most of what you do is worthy of a man.

We ought to live with the gods. This is done by being contented with the appointment of providence and by obeying the orders of that divinity which is God's deputy; and this divine authority is no more or less than that soul and reason which every man carries within him.

VI-Of Liberality in Outlook

The best way of revenge is not to imitate the injury. Be always doing something serviceable to mankind; and let this constant generosity be your pleasure, not forgetting a due regard to God.

The world is either an aggregation of atoms, or it is a unity ruled by law and providence. If the first, what should I stay for, where nature is a chaos and things are blindly jumbled together? But if there is a providence, I adore the great Governor of the world, and am at ease and cheerful in the prospect of protection.

Suppose you had a stepmother and a mother at the same time; though you would pay regard to the first, your converse would be principally with the latter. Let the court and philosophy represent these two relations to me.

If an antagonist in the circus tears our flesh with his nails, or tilts against us with his head, we do not cry out foul play, nor are we offended, nor do we suspect him afterwards as a dangerous person. Let us act thus in the other instances of life. When we receive a blow, let us think that we are but at a trial of skill and depart without malice or ill will.

It is enough to do my duty; as for other things, I will not be disturbed about them.

The vast continents of Europe and of Asia are but corners of the creation; the ocean is but a drop, and Mount Athos but a grain in respect of the universe; and the present instant of time is but a point to the extent of eternity.

When you have a mind to divert your fancy, try to consider the good qualities of your acquaintance—such as the enterprising vigour of this man, the modesty of another, the liberality of a third, and so on. Let this practice be always at hand.

VII-Of Patience and Toleration

What is wickedness? It is nothing new. When you are in danger of being shocked, consider that the sight is nothing but what you have frequently seen already. All ages and histories, towns and families, are full of the same stories; there is nothing new to be met with, but all things are common and quickly over.

Nature works up the matter of the universe like wax; now it is a horse; soon you will find it melted down and run into the figure of a tree, then a man, then something else. Only for a brief time is it fixed in any species.

Antisthenes said: 'It is the fate of princes to be ill spoken of for their good deeds.'

Consider the course of the stars as if you were driving through the sky and kept them company. Such contemplations as these scour off the rust contracted by conversing here below.

Rational creatures are designed for the advantage of each other. A sociable temper is that for which human nature was principally intended.

It is a saying of Plato's that no one misses the truth by his own goodwill. The same may be said of honesty, sobriety, good nature and the like. Remember this for it will help to sweeten your temper.

Though the gods are immortal, and have had their patience tried through so many ages, yet they even provide liberally for us. And are you tired with evil men already, who are an unhappy mortal yourself?

VIII-Of the Triple Responsibility

Every man has three relations to acquit himself in; his body, God, and his neighbours.

Have you seen a hand or a foot cut off and removed from the body? Just such a thing is the man who is discontented with destiny or cuts himself off by selfishness from the interest of mankind. But here is the fortunate aspect of the case—it lies in his power to set the limb on again. Consider the peculiar bounty of God to man in this privilege: He has set him above the necessity of breaking off from nature and providence at all; but supposing this misfortune to have occurred, it is in man's power to rejoin the body, and grow together again.

Do not take your whole life into your head at a time, nor burden yourself with the weight of the future. Neither what is past nor what is to come need afflict you, for you have only to deal with the present; and this is strangely lessened if you take it singly and by itself. Chide your fancy, therefore, if it grow faint.

Throw me into what climate or state you please, for all that I will keep my soul content. Is any misadventure big enough to ruffle my peace, or to make my mind mean, craving and servile? What is there that can justify such disorders?

Be not heavy in business, nor disturbed in conversation, nor rambling in thought. Do not burden yourself with too much employment. Do men curse you? This cannot prevent you from keeping a wise, temperate and upright mind. If a man standing by a lovely spring should rail at it, the water is none the worse for his foul language; and if he throw in dirt it will soon disappear and the fountain will be as wholesome as ever. How are you to keep your springs always running, that they may never stagnate into a pool? You must persevere in the virtues of freedom, sincerity, moderation and good nature.

IX-Of Moderation in Deed and Wish

Do not drudge like a galley-slave, nor do business in a laborious manner, as if you wish to be pitied or wondered at.

As virtue and vice consist in action, and not in the impressions of the senses, so it is not what they feel, but what they do, that makes mankind happy or miserable.

This man prays that he may gain such a woman; but do you rather pray that you may have no such inclination. Another invokes the gods to set him free from some troublesome circumstance; but let it be your petition that your mind may not be set upon such a wish. A third is devout in order to prevent the loss of his son; but I would have you pray rather against the fear of losing him. Let this be the rule for your devotions, and watch the event.

X-Of Sincerity and its Rewards

O My soul, are you ever to be rightly good, sincere and uniform, and made more visible to yourself than the body that hangs about you? Are you ever likely to relish good nature and general kindness as you ought? Will you ever be fully satisfied, rise above wanting and wishing, and never desire to obtain your pleasure out of anything foreign, either living or inanimate? Are you ever likely to be so happily qualified as to converse with the gods and men in such a manner as neither to complain of them nor to be condemned by them?

Put it out of the power of all men to give you a bad name, and if anyone reports you not to be an honest or a good man let your practice give him the lie. This is quite feasible; for who can hinder you from being just and sincere?

There is no one so happy in his family and friends but that some of them, when they see him going, will rejoice at a good riddance. Let him be a person of never so much probity and prudence, yet someone will say at his grave: 'Well, our man of order and gravity is gone; we shall be no more troubled with his discipline.' This is the best treatment a good man must expect.

XI-Of Calmness under Ill Usage

What a brave soul it is that is always ready to depart from the body and is unconcerned as to whether she will be extinguished, scattered, or removed! But she must be prepared upon reasonable grounds, and not out of mere obstinacy like the Christians; her fortitude must have nothing of noise or of tragic ostentation, but must be grave and seemly.

How fulsome and hollow does that man seem who cries: 'I'm resolved to deal sincerely with you!' Hark you, friend, what need of all this flourish? Let your actions speak. Your face ought to vouch for you. I would have virtue look out of the eye no less apparently than love does. A man of integrity and good nature can never be concealed, for his character is wrought into his countenance.

Gentleness and good humour are invincible, provided they are of the right stamp and without hypocrisy. This is the way to disarm the most outrageous person—to continue kind and unmoved under ill usage and to strike in at the right opportunity with advice. But let all be done out of mere love and kindness.

XII-The Fortitude that is Roman

I have often wondered how it is that everyone should love himself best and yet value his neighbour's opinion of him more than his own. If any man should be ordered to turn his inside outwards and publish every thought and fancy as fast as they came into his head, he would not submit to so much as a day of this discipline. Thus it is that we dread our neighbour's judgment more than our own.

What a mighty privilege man is born to, since it is in his power not to do anything but what God Almighty approves, and to be satisfied with all the distributions of providence!

Reflect upon those who have made the most glorious figure or have met with the greatest misfortunes. Where are they all now? They are vanished like a little smoke; they are nothing but ashes, and a tale— or not even a tale. Recollect likewise everything of this sort: what Fabius Catullinus did at his country seat; Lucius Lupus, in his garden; Stertinius, at Baiae; Tiberius, at Capreae; Rufus, at Velia: in short, the overweening importance attached to anything whatsover. The prize is insignificant and the game not worth the candle. It is much more becoming to a philosopher to stand clear of affection, to be honest and moderate upon all occasions and to follow cheerfully wherever the gods lead on, remembering that nothing is more scandalous than a man who is proud of his humility.

Listen, friend! You have been a burgher of this great city. What matter though you have lived in it fewer years or more? If you have kept the laws of the corporation, the length or shortness of the time makes no difference. Where is the hardship, then, if nature, that planted you here, orders your removal? You cannot say you are sent off by an unjust tyrant. No! You quit the stage as fairly as a player does who has his discharge from the master of the revels.

'But I have only gone through three acts, and not held out to the end of the fifth!'

True; but in life three acts may complete the play. He is the only judge of completeness who first ordered your entrance and now orders your exit; you are accountable for neither the one nor the other. Retire, therefore, in serenity, as He who dismisses you is serene.

AUGUSTINE

(354-430)

"I heard from a neighbouring house a voice as of a boy or girl, I know not, chanting, and oft repeating, take up and read; take up and read."

Augustine, born in North Africa in 354, would become one of the most important influences on the early Christian church. Augustine described his early life as one of sin and general debauchery. His early religious stirrings brought him into contact with the Manicheans, which he eventually rejected in favor of Neo-Platonism. It was Neo-Platonism that provided Augustine with the foundations of his Christian philosophy.

Augustine set forth his intellectual and spiritual path in *The Confessions*, in which he acknowledges his errant ways and proceeds to describe his path to spiritual enlightenment. The early chapters of the book deal with his childhood, his relationship with his mother, and his eventual conversion to the Christian faith at age thirty-two.

The last chapters of *The Confessions* represent Augustine's attempt to explain the Old Testament view of creation. Throughout the text, which is addressed to God, Augustine uses prayers, meditations, and instructions. These interspersions themselves, have become tremendously influential on the Christian Church.

The Confessions constitutes a moving description of one man's journey to grace. Augustine's profound influence on Christian philosophy was greater than that of any other early church father. Readers of *The Confessions* should be aware of the influence of Platonic thought on the writings of Augustine. *The Confessions*, in many ways, represents the blending of philosophy with the Christian faith.

Plato, along with the Apostle Paul, represents a key influence on Augustine, and therefore on the development of Western thought.

CONFESSIONS

ST. AUGUSTINE

I-Regrets for a Mis-Spent Youth

Great art Thou, O Lord, and greatly to be praised. My faith, Lord, should call on Thee, which Thou hast given me by the incarnation of Thy Son, through the ministry of the preacher, Ambrose. How shall I call upon my God? What room is there within me, wherein my God can come? Narrow is the house of my soul; enlarge Thou it, that it may be able to receive Thee. Thou madest us for Thyself, and our hearts are restless until they rest in Thee.

I began, as yet a boy, to pray to Thee, that I might not be beaten at school; but I sinned in disobeying the commands of parents and teachers through love of play, delighting in the pride of victory in my contests. I loved not study, and hated to be forced to it. Unless forced, I did not learn at all. But no one does well against his will, even though what he does is good. But what was well came to me from Thee, my God, for Thou hast decreed that every inordinate affection should carry with it its own punishment.

But why did I so much hate the Greek which I was taught as a boy? I do not yet fully know. For the Latin I loved; not what my first masters, but what the so-called grammarians taught me. For those first lessons—reading, writing and arithmetic—I thought as great a burden and as vexatious as any Greek. But in the other lessons I learnt the wanderings of Aeneas, forgetful of my own, and wept for the dead Dido because she killed herself for love; while, with dry eyes, I endured my miserable self-dying among these things, far from Thee, my God, my life.

Why, then, did I hate the Greek classics, full of like fiction to those in Virgil? For Homer also curiously wove similar stories, and is most pleasant, yet was disagreeable to my boyish taste. In truth, the difficulty of a foreign tongue dashed as with gall all the sweetness of the Greek fable. For not one word of it did I understand, and to make me learn I was urged vehemently with cruel threats and stripes. Yet I learnt with delight the fictions in Latin concerning the wicked doings of Jove and Juno, and for this I was pronounced a hopeful boy, being applauded above many of my own age and class.

I will now call to mind my past uncleanness and the carnal corruptions of my soul; not because I love them, but that I may love Thee, O my God. What was it that I delighted in, but to love and to be beloved? But I kept not the measure of love, of soul to soul, friendship's bright boundary, for I could not discern the brightness of love from the fog of lust. Where was I, and how far was I exiled from the delights of Thy house, in that sixteenth year of my age, when the madness of licence took the rule over me? My friends, meanwhile, took no care by marriage to prevent my fall; their only care was that I should learn to speak excellently and become a great orator.

Now, for that year my studies were intermitted; whilst, after my return from Madaura—a neighbouring city whither I had journeyed to learn grammar and rhetoric—the expenses for a further journey to Carthage were provided for me; and that rather by sacrifice than by the ordinary means of my father, who was but a poor freeman of Tagaste. But yet this same father had no concern how I grew towards Thee; or how chaste I were; or, so that I were but eloquent, how barren I were to Thy culture, O God.

But while in that my sixteenth year I lived with my parents, the briers of unclean desires grew rank over my head and there was no hand to root them out. My father rejoiced to see me growing towards manhood, but in my mother's breast Thou hadst already begun Thy temple, whereas my father was as yet but a catechumen, and that but recently.

I remember how she, seized with a holy fear and trembling, in private warned me with great anxiety against fornication. These seemed to me womanish advices which I should blush to obey. But they were Thine, and I knew it not. I ran headlong with such blindness that amongst my equals I was ashamed of being less shameless than others when I heard them boast of their wickedness. I would even say I had done what I had not done that I might not seem contemptible in proportion as I was innocent.

II-Monica's Prayers and Augustine's Paganism

To Carthage I came, where there sang in my ears a cauldron of unholy loves. I defiled the spring of friendship with the filth of concupiscence, and I beclouded its brightness with the hell of lust.

Stage plays also carried me away, full of images of my miseries and of fuel to my fire. In the theatres I rejoiced with lovers, when they succeeded in their criminal intrigues, imaginary only in the play; and when they lost one another I sorrowed with them. Those studies also which were accounted commendable, led me away, having a view of excelling in the courts of litigation, where I should be the more praised the craftier I became. And now I was head scholar in the rhetoric school, whereat I swelled with conceit. I learnt books of eloquence, wherein I desired to be eminent.

In the course of study I fell upon a certain book of Cicero which contains an exhortation to philosophy, and is called 'Hortensius'. This book changed my disposition, and turned my prayers to Thyself, O Lord. I longed with an incredible ardour for the immortality of wisdom and began now to arise a wish that I might return to Thee. I resolved then to turn my mind to the Holy Scriptures, to see what they were; but when I turned to them my pride shrank from their humility, disdaining to be one of the little ones, to whom they are laid open.

Therefore, I fell among men proudly doting, exceeding carnal and great talkers, who served up to me, when hungering after thee, the Sun and Moon, beautiful works of Thine, but not Thyself. Yet, taking these glittering fantasies to be Thee, I fed thereon, but was not nourished. I knew not God to be a Spirit. Nor knew I that true inward righteousness, which judgeth not according to custom, but out of the most righteous law of Almighty God. Under the influence of these Manichaeans I scoffed at Thy holy servants and prophets. And Thou 'sentest Thine hand from above,' and deliveredst my soul from that profound darkness.

My mother, Thy faithful one, wept to Thee for me, for she discerned the death wherein I lay, and Thou heardest her, O Lord. Thou gavest her answers first in visions. There passed yet nine years in which I wallowed in the mire of that deep pit and the darkness of error.

Thou gavest her meantime another answer by a priest of Thine, a certain bishop brought up in Thy Church, and well studied in books, whom she entreated to converse with me and to refute my errors. He answered that I was as yet unteachable, being puffed up with the novelty of that heresy. 'But let him alone awhile,' saith he; 'only pray to God for him, he will of himself, by reading, find what that error is, and how great its impiety.'

He told her how he himself, when a little one, had by his mother been consigned over to the Manichaeans, but had found out how much that sect was to be abhorred and had, therefore, avoided it. But he assured her that the child of such tears as hers could not perish. Which answer she took as an oracle from heaven.

Thus, from my nineteenth year to my twenty-eighth we lived, hunting after popular applause and poetic prizes, and secretly following a false religion. In those years I taught rhetoric, and in those years I had conversation with one—not in that which is called lawful marriage—yet with but one, remaining faithful even unto her. Those impostors whom they style astrologers I consulted without scruple.

In those years, when I first began to teach rhetoric in my native town, I had made one my friend, only too dear to me from a community of studies and pursuits, of my own age and, as myself, in the first bloom of youth. I had perverted him also to those superstitions and pernicious fables for which my mother bewailed me. With me he now erred in mind, nor could my soul be happy without him. But behold Thou wert close on the steps of Thy fugitives, at once 'God of Vengeance' and Fountain of Mercies, turning us to Thyself by wonderful means.

Thou tookest that man out of this life, when he had scarce filled up one whole year of my friendship, sweet to me above all sweetness of that my life. For long, sore sick of a fever, he lay senseless in a death-sweat; so that, his recovery being despaired of, he was baptised in that condition. He was relieved and restored, and I essayed to jest with him, expecting him to do the same, at that baptism which he had received when in the swoon. But he shrank from me, and forbade such language.

A few days afterwards he was happily taken from my folly, that with Thee he might be preserved for my comfort. In my absence he was attacked again by the fever, and so died. At this grief my heart was utterly darkened. My native country was a torment, and my father's house a strange unhappiness to me. At length I fled out of my country, for so my eyes missed him less where they were wont to see him. And thus from Tagaste I came to Carthage.

III-The Influence of St. Ambrose on Augustine's Life

I would lay open before my God that nine and twentieth year of my age. There had then come to Carthage a certain Bishop of the Manichaeans, Faustus by name, a great snare of the Devil, and many were entangled by him through the smooth lure of his language. But it soon became clear that he was ignorant in those arts in which I thought he excelled, and I began to despair of his solving the difficulties which perplexed me. He was sensible of his ignorance in these things, and confessed it, and thus my zeal for the writings of the Manichaeans was blunted. Thus Faustus, to so many a snare of death, had now, neither willing nor witting it, begun to loosen that wherein I was taken.

Thou didst deal with me that I should be persuaded to go to Rome and to teach there rather what I was teaching at Carthage, my chief and only reason being that I heard that young men studied there more peacefully, and were kept under a more regular discipline. My mother remained behind weeping and praying. And, behold, at Rome I was received by the scourge of bodily sickness, and I was going down to hell, carrying all the sins that I had committed. Thou healedst me of that sickness that I might live for Thee to bestow upon me a better and more abiding health.

I began, then, diligently to teach rhetoric in Rome when, lo! I found other offences committed in that city, to which I had not been exposed in Africa, for, on a sudden, a number of youths plot together to avoid paying their master's salary and remove to another school. When, therefore, they of Milan had sent to Rome to the prefect of the city, to furnish them with a rhetoric reader for their city, I made application that Symmachus, then prefect of the city, would try me by setting me some subject for oration, and send me.

Thus to Milan I came, to Ambrose the bishop, best known to the whole world as among the best of men, Thy servant. To him I was unknowing led by Thee, that by him I might knowingly be led to Thee. That man of God received me as a father, and showed me an episcopal kindness on my coming. Thenceforth I began to love him. I was delighted with his eloquence as he preached to the people, though I took no pains to learn what he taught, but only to hear how he spake.

My mother had now come to me. When I had discovered to her that I was now no longer a Manichaean, though not yet a Catholic

Christian, she was not overjoyed, as at something unexpected. But she redoubled her prayers and tears for me now that what she had begged of Thee daily with tears was in so great part realized; and she hurried the more eagerly to the church, and hung on the lips of Ambrose, whom she loved as 'an angel of God,' because she knew that by him I had been brought to that wavering I was now in. I heard him every Lord's Day expound the word of truth, and was sure that all the knots of the Manichaeans could be unravelled. So I was confounded and converted. Yet I panted after honours, gains, marriage—and in these desires I underwent most bitter crosses.

Meantime my sins were being multiplied. Continual effort was made to have me married, chiefly through my mother's pains, that so once married, the health-giving baptism might cleanse me. My concubine being torn from my side as a hindrance to my marriage, my heart, which clave unto her, was torn; and she returned to Africa, leaving with me my son by her. But, unhappy, I procured another, though no wife.

To Thee be praise, to Thee be glory, Fountain of Mercies! I was becoming more miserable and Thou drewest nearer to me in my misery!

IV-The Birth of a New Life

My evil and abominable youth was now dead, and I was passing into early manhood. Meeting with certain books of the Platonists, translated from Greek into Latin, I therein read, not in the same words, but to the same purpose, that 'In the beginning was the Word, and the Word was with God, and the Word was God.' But that 'the Word was made flesh and dwelt among us' I read not there. That Jesus humbled Himself to the death of the Cross, and was raised from the dead and exalted unto glory, that at His name every knee should bow, I read not there.

Then I sought a way of obtaining strength, and found it not until I embraced 'that Mediator between God and Man, the Man Christ Jesus.' Eagerly did I seize that venerable writing of Thy Spirit, and chiefly the Apostle Paul. Whereupon those difficulties vanished wherein he formerly seemed to me to contradict himself and the text of his discourse not to agree with the testimonies of the Law and the Prophets. But now they appeared to me to contain one pure and uniform doctrine; and I learnt to 'rejoice with trembling.'

I had now found the goodly pearl, which, selling all I had, I ought to have bought, and I hesitated. To Simplicianus (sent from Rome to be an instructor and director of Ambrose) then I went, the spiritual Father of Ambrose and now a bishop, to whom I related the mazes of my wanderings. He testified his joy that I had read certain books of the Platonists and had not fallen on the writings of other deceitful philosophers.

And he related to me the story of the conversion of Victorinus, the translator of those Platonist books, who was not ashamed to become the humble little child of Thy Christ, after he had for years with thundering eloquence inspired the people with the love of Anubis, the barking deity, and all the monster gods who fought against Neptune, Venus and Minerva, so that Rome now adored the deities she had formerly conquered. But this proud worshipper of daemons suddenly and unexpectedly said to Simplicianus, 'Get us to the Church; I wish to be made a Christian.' And he was baptised, to the wonder of Rome and the joy of the Church.

I was fired by this story and longed now to devote myself entirely to God, but still did my two wills, one new and the other old, one carnal and the other spiritual, struggle within me; and by their discord undid my soul. And how Thou didst deliver me out of the bonds of desire, wherewith I was bound most straitly to carnal concupiscence, I will now declare and confess.

Upon a day there came to see me and Alypius one Pontitianus, an African fellow-countryman, in high office at the Emperor's court, who was a Christian and baptised. He told us how one afternoon at Triers, when the Emperor was taken up with the Circensian games, he and three companions went to walk in gardens near the city walls and lighted on a certain cottage, inhabited by certain of Thy servants, and there they found a little book containing the life of Antony. This some of them began to read and admire; and he, as he read, began to meditate on taking up such a life. By that book he was changed inwardly, as was one of his companions also. Both had affianced brides, who, when they heard of this change, dedicated their virginity to God.

V-God's Command to Augustine and the Death of Monica

After much soul-sickness and torment of spirit took place an incident by which Thou didst wholly break my chains. I was bewailing and weeping in my heart, when, lo! I heard from a neighbouring house a voice as of a boy or girl, I know not, chanting, and oft repeating 'Tolle, lege; tolle, lege' ['Take up and read; take up and read'].

Instantly I rose up, interpreting it to be no other than a command from God, to open the Book and read the first chapter I should find. Eagerly I seized the volume of the apostle and opened and read that section on which my eyes fell first: 'Not in rioting and drunkeness, not in chambering and wantonness, not in strife and envying; but put ye on the Lord Jesus Christ, and make no provision for the flesh, to fulfil the lusts thereof.' No further would I read, nor needed I, for a light as it were of serenity diffused in my heart, and all the darkness of doubt vanished away.

When shall I recall all that passed in those holy days? In the vintage vacation I gave notice to the Milanese to provide their scholars with another master to sell words to them; for I had made my choice to serve Thee. It pleased Alypius also, when the time was come for my baptism, to be born again with me in Thee. We joined with us the boy, Adeodatus, born to me, of my sin. Excellently hadst Thou made him. He was not quite fifteen, and in wit surpassed many grave and learned men. We were baptised, and anxiety for our past life vanished from us.

The time was now approaching when thy handmaid, my mother Monica, was to depart this life. She fell sick of a fever, and on the ninth day of that sickness, and the fifty-sixth year of her age, and the three and thirtieth of mine, was that religious and holy soul set free from that body. Being thus forsaken of so great comfort in her, my soul was wounded. Little by little the wound was healed as I recovered my former thoughts of her holy conversation towards Thee and her holy tenderness and observance towards us. May she rest in peace, with her husband Patricius, whom she obeyed, 'with patience bringing forth fruit' unto Thee, that she might win him also unto Thee.

This is the object of my confessions of what I am now, not of what I have been—to confess this not before Thee only, but in the ears also of the believing sons of men. Too late I loved Thee! Thou wast with me, but I was not with Thee. And now my whole hope is in nothing but Thy great mercy.

Since Thou gavest me continency I have observed it; but I retain the memory of evil habits, and their images come up oft before me. And thou hast taught me concerning eating and drinking, that I should set myself to take food as medicine. I strive daily against concupiscence in eating and drinking. Thou hast disentangled me from the delight of the ear and from the lusts of the eye. Into many snares of the senses my mind wanders miserably, but Thou pluckest me out mercifully.

By pride, vainglory and love of praise I am tempted, but I seek Thy mercy till what is lacking in me by Thee be renewed and perfected. Thou knowest my unskilfulness; teach me the wondrous things out of Thy law and heal me.

FRANCIS BACON

(1561-1626)

"There are four classes of idols which beset men's minds. To these, for distinction's sake, I have assigned names, – calling the first class Idols of the Tribe; the second, Idols of the Cave; the third, Idols of the Market-place; the fourth, Idols of the Theater.

Along with René Descartes Sir Francis Bacon was one of the wellsprings of modern thought. A man of diverse interests—science, politics, literature—Bacon sought to bring to an end the stifling authority of the past, arguing that "knowledge is power" and that the benefits to be derived from such power were being denied to human beings by their submission to the false and outdated concepts of an unscientific intellectual tradition.

In his *Novum Organum* (New Method) he attacked what he believed to be the false idols that dominate and restrict human understanding.

NOVUM ORGANUM

FRANCIS BACON

xxxvii

The doctrine of those who have denied that certainty could be attained at all, has some agreement with my way of proceeding at the first setting out; but they end in being infinitely separated and opposed. For the holders of that doctrine assert simply that nothing can be known; I also assert that not much can be known in nature by the way which is now in use. But then they go on to destroy the authority of the senses and understanding; whereas I proceed to devise and supply helps for the same.

xxxviii

The idols and false notions which are now in possession of the human understanding, and have taken deep root therein, not only so beset men's minds that truth can hardly find entrance, but even after entrance obtained, they will again in the very instauration of the sciences meet and trouble us, unless men being forewarned of the danger fortify themselves as far as may be against their assaults.

xxxix

There are four classes of idols which beset men's minds. To these for distinction's sake I have assigned names,—calling the first class *Idols of the Tribe;* the second, *Idols of the Cave;* the third, *Idols of the Marketplace;* the fourth, *Idols of the Theater.*

xl

The formation of ideas and axioms by true induction is no doubt the proper remedy to be applied for the keeping off and clearing away of idols. To point them out, however, is of great use, for the doctrine of idols is to the interpretation of nature what the doctrine of the refutation of sophisms is to common logic.

xli

The Idols of the Tribe have their foundation in human nature itself, and in the tribe or race of men. For it is a false assertion that the sense of man is the measure of things. On the contrary, all perceptions, as well of the sense as of the mind, are according to the measure of the individual and not according to the measure of the universe. And the human understanding is like a false mirror, which, receiving rays irregularly, distorts and discolors the nature of things by mingling its own nature with it.

xlii

The Idols of the Cave are the idols of the individual man. For everyone (besides the errors common to human nature in general) has a cave or den of his own, which refracts and discolors the light of nature; owing either to his own proper and peculiar nature or to his education and conversation with others; or to the reading of books, and the authority of those whom he esteems and admires; or to the differences of impressions, accordingly as they take place in a mind preoccupied and predisposed or in a mind indifferent and settled; or the like. So that the spirit of man (according as it is meted out to different individuals) is in fact a thing variable and full of perturbation, and governed as it were by chance. Whence it was well observed by Heraclitus that men look for sciences in their own lesser worlds, and not in the greater or common world.

xliii

There are also idols formed by the intercourse and association of men with each other, which I call Idols of the Market-place, on account of the commerce and consort of men there. For it is by discourse that men associate; and words are imposed according to the apprehension of the vulgar. And therefore the ill and unfit choice of words wonderfully obstructs the understanding. Nor do the definitions or explanations wherewith in some things learned men are wont to guard and defend themselves, by any means set the matter right. But words plainly force and overrule the understanding, and throw all into confusion, and lead men away into numberless empty controversies and idle fancies.

xliv

Lastly, there are idols which have immigrated into men's minds from the various dogmas of philosophies, and also from wrong laws of demonstration. These I call Idols of the Theater: because in my judgment all the received systems are but so many stage-plays, representing worlds of their own creation after an unreal and scenic fashion. Nor is it only of the systems now in vogue, or only of the ancient sects and philosophies, that I speak: for many more plays of the same kind may yet be composed and in like artificial manner set forth: seeing that errors the most widely different have nevertheless causes for the most part alike. Neither again do I mean this only of entire systems, but also of many principles and axioms in science. Which by tradition, credulity, and negligence have come to be received.

But of these several kinds of idols I must speak more largely and exactly, that the understanding may be duly cautioned.

THOMAS HOBBES

(1588-1679)

"So men invade each other, first for gain, second for safety, and third for reputation."

Thomas Hobbes came of age in one of the most turbulent periods in English history. He would live to see the execution of King Charles I in 1649, the rule of Oliver Cromwell, and eventually the restoration of the Stuart monarchy in Charles II (1660). Consequently, Hobbes developed a secular view of history. His chief aim was to provide a justification for the political state. Amid the chaos of his time, he advocated rule by an absolute sovereign. In Hobbes's view, only a state ruled by an absolute power could bring order to England.

Hobbes's *Leviathan*, written in 1651, is his best known work. The title itself gives direct insight into the type of political state advocated by Hobbes. Leviathan is drawn from the *Old Testament* and refers to a great sea monster. Hobbes intended for his absolute government to be a sort of all-controlling monster. He weighs against democracy as being too cumbersome and inadequate to control the basic desires of mankind. Only an absolute ruler with complete authority could rein in the greed and lust of the people. It is important to note that Hobbes does not necessarily favor a monarchy over other types of dictatorial rule. By sovereign he refers to any ruler who maintains law and order. His sovereign may be a king or a dictator such as Oliver Cromwell.

Another important aspect of Hobbes's *Leviathan* is his espousal of the social contract. The social contract, as described by Hobbes, represents the agreement between the people and the absolute ruler. The people give up a large measure of personal liberty in exchange for order and protection. Hobbes viewed the social contract as inviolable as long as life and property are defended by the absolute ruler.

Hobbes's *Leviathan* stands with Machiavelli's *The Prince* as one of the most important political treatises of the early modern period. He would inspire such thinkers as John Locke, Montesquieu, and Jean Jacques Rousseau to develop their own versions of the social contract.

LEVIATHAN

THOMAS HOBBES

I-Of Man

Nature, the art whereby God hath made and governs the world, is by the art of man so imitated that he can make an artificial animal. For by art is created that great leviathan called a commonwealth or state, which is but an artificial man; in which the sovereignty is an artificial soul, as giving life and motion; the magistrates and other officers the joints; reward and punishment the nerves; concord, health; discord, sickness; lastly, the pacts or covenants by which the parts were first set together resemble the 'fiat' of God at the Creation.

To describe this artificial man, I will consider: First, the matter and the artificer, both which is man; secondly, how it is made; thirdly, what is a Christian commonwealth; lastly, what is the kingdom of darkness.

And first, of man. The thoughts of man are, singly, every one a representation of some quality or accident of a body without us, called an object. There is no conception in the mind which has not first been begotten upon the organs of sense. The cause of sense is the eternal object which presseth upon the proper organ; not that, as hath been taught in the schools, the thing 'sendeth forth a visible or audible species.'

Imagination is the continuity of an image after the object is removed. When we would express that the image is decaying, we call it memory; in sleep, we call it dreams.

Of all invention, the most notable is that of speech, names, the register of thoughts; which are notes for remembrance, or signs, for transference. Truth consisteth in the right ordering of names in our affirmations. Words are wise men's counters, but the money of fools.

Reasoning is the reckoning, the addition and subtraction of the sequences of words, the sum being the conclusion. Which conclusions may be absurd, because men do not start—except in geometry—from the definitions of the words. Reason, therefore, implies speech.

In animals there are two sorts of motions—vital and voluntary. The beginnings of motion within man are called 'endeavour.' Appetite is a motion towards; aversion is a motion fromwards. Some are born in us, some are products of experience. The object of a man's appetite he calls 'good'; of his aversion, 'evil'; whether in promise (beautiful and ugly), in effect (pleasant, painful), or as means (useful, hurtful). Pleasures and pains arise from an object present, of the senses; or in expectation, of the mind. Thus 'pity' is the imagining of a like calamity befalling oneself.

'Deliberation' is the sum of the successive appetites or aversions which are concluded by the doing or not doing of the particular thing. 'Will' is the last appetite in deliberating. So, in the enquiry of the truth, opinions correspond to appetites, and the final judgement, the last opinion, to the will.

There are two kinds of knowledge; of 'fact' and of 'the consequence of one affirmation to another.' The former is nothing else but sense and memory, and is absolute; the latter is called science, and is conditional. The register of the first is called history, natural or civil; that of the second is contained in books of philosophy, in corresponding groups—natural philosophy, and civil philosophy or politics. Natural philosophy breaks up into a number of groups, including mental and moral science.

Power is present means, whencesoever derived, to attain some future apparent good. Value is the price that will be given for the use of a man's power. To honour a man is to acknowledge his power; to dishonour him is to depreciate it. The public worth of a man is the value set on him by the commonwealth.

By manners, I mean those qualities of mankind which are concerned with their living together in peace and unity. Desire of power tends to produce strife; other desires, as for ease, or for knowledge, incline men to obey a common power. To receive benefits, or to do injuries, greater than can be repaid or expiated, tends to make us hate the benefactor or the injured party.

II-Of Contract and Sovereignty

Nature hath made men so equal, in the faculties of body and mind that are born in them, that one man cannot in respect of these claim to himself any benefit to which another may not pretend. From this equality ariseth equality of hope in the attaining of our ends. Therefore, if two men desire the same thing which they cannot both enjoy they become enemies, and seek each the destruction of the other, each mistrusting the other. So men invade each other, first for gain, second for safety, and third for reputation.

Hence, while men live without a common power to keep them all in awe, they are in a state of war, every man against every man. In this state, notions of right and wrong, justice and injustice, have no place. Probably there never was actually such an universal condition; but we see it now among savage races and in the mutual relations of sovereigns. In this state of war, reason suggesteth articles of peace upon which men may agree; which articles are otherwise called the laws of nature.

The right 'of nature' is the right of self-preservation. 'Liberty' is the absence of impediments to the exercise of power. A 'law of nature' is a precept of reason forbidding a man to do what is destructive of his own life. In the state of nature every man has a 'right' to everything. Thus security comes only of the first fundamental law: 'To seek peace and follow it,' and 'by all means we can defend ourselves.'

The second law follows: 'To lay down the right to everything, claiming only so much against others as we concede to others against ourselves.' This right being renounced or transferred, injustice is the revocation of that act. But since the object of a voluntary act is good to oneself, such renunciation is not valid if not good for oneself; hence a man cannot renounce the right of self-preservation.

The transferring of right, if not mutual, is free gift; if mutual, it is contract. When this is not simultaneous there is a covenant or pact. The covenant can become void only through some new fact arising after it was made. A covenant not to defend oneself against force by force is void *per se*.

The third law is: 'That men perform their covenant, made,' without which covenants are vain, and the state of war continues. The definition of injustice is 'the not-performance of a covenant.' No covenant is valid until there exists some power that can enforce the performance of it by penalties; that is, until there is a commonwealth. What is done to a man conformable to his own will signified to the doer is no injury to him.

The fourth law is that of 'gratitude'; that a man receiving a free gift endeavour that the giver may not suffer thereby. A fifth is 'conplaisance'—that every man strive to accommodate himself to the rest. Others are pardon on repentance, and nonvindictiveness of punishment; and the common enjoyment—or, failing that, distribution by lot—of what cannot be equally divided.

Persons are either natural and actual, or fictitious and artificial, *i.e.,* representing someone else, or even something else: as a church, a hospital, a bridge. When the representative has authority from the represented, we call the former the 'actor,' and the latter the 'author.' One person may artificially represent a multitude.

Now, men being in the state of nature may agree together; but there is no security, unless there be a power to enforce the covenant. Such a power can be created only if they agree together to confer all their own power on one man or one assembly; so that all the acts of such person or assembly have authority as from each one of them, and each one of them submits his individual will to that of such person or assembly. The multitude so united in one person is a commonwealth. This is the generation of that leviathan or mortal god to which, under the Immortal God, we owe our peace and defence.

He that carrieth this person is called 'sovereign,' and everyone beside is his 'subject.' This sovereign power may be attained either by natural force, 'acquisition,' or by voluntary 'institution.'

They that have instituted a commonwealth by covenant cannot make a new covenant contrary thereto without permission of the sovereign, since this is a breaking of their covenant with each other. On his part there is no covenant, so that breach of covenant by him cannot be pleaded as warranting abrogation of the covenant made. The sovereign cannot do the subjects injustice because, since he has their authority, what he does to them is done by their own will; so also they cannot punish him.

Since the sovereign was instituted for peace and defence, he controls the means to war and peace, and judges of opinions as conducing to peace or endangering it. He prescribes the rules of property, since in the state of nature there is no property; he has the right of adjudicature; of making war and peace with other commonwealths; of choosing all counsellors in peace and war; of rewarding and punishing, according to the law he has made and of bestowing honour. Nay, if he grants away any of these powers the grant is null.

The sovereignty may be in one man, or in a limited assembly, or in an assembly of all—monarchy, aristocracy, democracy; these three forms only, though when they are misliked they are called other names. In any case, the power of the sovereign is absolute, whether a monarch or an assembly. He is the representative of the commonwealth, not deputies who may be chosen to tender positions.

The three forms differ not in the power of the sovereign, but in their advantageousness. In monarchy, the private interest of the sovereign must coincide with that of the commonwealth as a whole; much more so than in aristocracy or democracy. An assembly cannot receive counsel secretly; a monarchy has the benefit of a single will instead of conflicting wills. There is no government by the mixture of the types, *e.g.,* an elective 'king' is not a sovereign, but a minister.

Men submit themselves to an instituted sovereign, for fear of each other; to an acquired sovereignty, for fear of the sovereign. Acquired sovereignty or dominion is either by generation (paternal) or by conquest. A family, however, does not amount to a commonwealth, unless it be so great that it may not be subdued by war. Acquired sovereignty is absolute for the same reasons as instituted sovereignty.

III-The Natural Commonwealth

Liberty is absence of impediments to motion. It is consistent with fear, also with necessity; for a voluntary act is yet necessary as having a cause which is a link in a chain of causes up to the First Cause, which is God. But men have created artificial impediments or bonds called laws. The liberty of the subject lies only in such things as the sovereign has permitted, for he hath power to regulate all, even life and death, at his own will. The liberty praised in Rome and Athens was the liberty of the commonwealth as against other commonwealths.

The subject has liberty to disobey the sovereign's command if it contravene the law that the right of self-preservation cannot be abrogated, unless it be to endanger himself for the preservation of the commonwealth, as with soldiers. The subjects' obligation of obedience lasts so long as the sovereign's power of defending them, that being the purpose of his being made sovereign.

By systems I mean numbers of men joined in one interest. These are political, constituted by law; and private, permitted or forbidden by law. All, except a commonwealth, are subordinate to the commonwealth, and have not the character of sovereignty. The rights of governing bodies are only those expressly conceded by law, either generally or to them specifically. Systems in the commonwealth correspond to muscles in the natural body.

The nourishment of the commonwealth is its commodities or products, the distribution of which must be at the will of the sovereign, whether of land or of commodities, exchanged internally or trafficked abroad.

The procreation, or children, of a commonwealth are its 'plantations,' or 'colonies,' which may be commonwealths themselves, as children emancipated, or remain parts of the commonwealth.

By civil laws I mean those laws that men are bound to obey as members of any commonwealth. The sovereign is the sole legislator, and is not subject to the laws which he can repeal at pleasure. The civil laws are the laws of nature expressed as commands of the commonwealth, or the will of the sovereign so expressed; whatever is not the law of nature must be expressly made known and published. Both the law of nature and written law require interpretation, which is by sentence of the judge constituted by sovereign authority.

An intention of breaking the law is a sin; issuing in a breach of the law it is crime. Violation of the laws of nature is always and everywhere sin; it is crime only when a violation of the laws of a commonwealth. Unavoidable ignorance of a law is a complete excuse for breaking it, but ignorance due to lack of diligence is not unavoidable. Terror of present death, or the order of the sovereign, is a complete excuse. And many circumstances may serve as extenuation.

A punishment is an evil inflicted by public authority on him that hath done or omitted that which is said to be by the same authority a transgression of the law, to the end that the will of men may thereby be the better disposed to obedience. Now, this right of punishment is not transferred by the subjects to the sovereign, since they cannot surrender their right of self-defence against violence. But as all before had the natural right of hurting others, that right is left by the covenant to the sovereign alone, strengthened by the resignation thereof by the rest.

Punishments inflicted by man are 'corporal' or 'pecuniary,' or 'ignominy,' or 'imprisonment,' or 'exile,' or mixed of these. Corporal are capital, with or without torment, and less than capital. Pecuniary includes deprivation not only of money but also of lands or other saleable goods; but such deprivation, if it is by way of compensation to the person injured, is not really punishment. Imprisonment, when it is only for the custody of a person accused, is not punishment. Exile is not so much a punishment as a command or permission to escape punishment, except when accompanied by deprivation of goods.

Infirmities of a commonwealth arise—from the first institution, when the sovereign has not assumed sufficient power; from such doctrines as that each man privately is the judge of good or evil actions, or sins if he obey the commonwealth against his 'conscience'; that the sovereign is subject to the civil laws; that private property excludes sovereign rights; that sovereign power may be divided, which is the worst of all; and from other causes, as of money grudged for wars; monopolies, over-potent subjects or corporation, insatiable desire of dominion. But when a country is conquered, that is the dissolution of the commonwealth.

Of the sovereign's duties the first is to surrender none of his powers, and the second to see that they be known, to which end, and the understanding of it, the people must be rightly instructed. Further, that he administer justice equally to all people, and impose equal taxes, and make good laws (I say good, not just, since no law can be unjust), and choose good counsellors.

Subjects owe simple obedience to the sovereign in all things whatsover, except what is contrary to the laws of God. Therefore, it remains here to speak of the kingdom of God, Whose subjects are they that believe in Him. God declareth His laws either by natural reason, or by revelation, or by the voice of prophets. He is necessarily sovereign, for the one reason that He is omnipotent.

IV-Of A Christian Commonwealth

Of God speaking by the voice of a prophet are two signs: that the prophet worketh miracles, and that he teacheth no other religion than that established. These two must go together. And since miracles have ceased, it is clear that God no longer speaks by prophets.

But He hath revealed Himself in Scripture—that is, in those books which are in the canon ordained. But whether their authority be derived from the civil sovereignty or is of a universal church to which all sovereigns are subordinate is another question. It may be seen, however, from Scripture that the kingdom of God therein spoken of is a civil kingdom, which is that kingdom of God by Christ which was interrupted by the revolt of the Israelites and the election of Saul.

A church is a term used in many senses, but in one only can it be treated as a person having power to will, command, or do any action whatever. And according to this sense I define a church to be 'a company of men professing Christian religion, united in the person of one sovereign at whose command they ought to assemble, and without whose authority they ought not to assemble.' It follows that a church that is assembled in any commonwealth that hath forbidden them to assemble is an unlawful assembly.

There are Christians in the dominions of several princes and states; but every one of them is subject to that commonwealth of which he is himself a member, and consequently cannot be subject to the commands of any other person. There is therefore no such universal church as all are bound to obey.

The original covenant with Abraham gave him the sole right, which is the inheritance of every sovereign, to punish any subject who should pretend to a private vision for the countenancing of any doctrine which Abraham should forbid. This covenant established that kingdom of God which was interrupted by the secular kingdom of Saul. The coming of Christ was to restore that kingdom by a new covenant; which kingdom was to be in another world after the Resurrection. The power ecclesiastical was left by Him to the apostles, but manifestly not a coercive power on earth, as Christ's own power on earth was not.

Christ, therefore, by His coming did not withdraw any of the power from civil sovereigns, and if they do commit the government of their subjects in matter of religion to the Pope, he holdeth that charge not as being above the civil sovereign, but by his authority.

But as for disagreement between the laws of God and the civil laws of the sovereign, the laws of God, which must in no wise be disobeyed, are those which are necessary to salvation; and these are summed up in the will to obey the law of God and the belief that Jesus is the Christ. But the private man may not set up to judge whether the ordinance of the sovereign be against the law of God or whether the doctrine which he imposeth consist with the belief that Jesus is the Christ.

But in the Scripture there is mention also of another power, the kingdom of Satan, 'the prince of the powers of the air,' which is a confederacy of deceivers that, 'to obtain dominion over men in this present world, endeavours by dark and erroneous doctrines to extinguish in them the light both of nature and of the Gospel, and so to disprepare them for the kingdom of God to come.'

And such darkness is wrought first by abusing the light of the Scriptures so that we know them not; secondly by introducing the demonology of the heathen poets; thirdly, by mixing with the Scripture divers relics of the religion and much of the erroneous philosophy of the Greeks; and, fourthly, by mingling with these false or uncertain traditions and feigned or uncertain history.

RENÉ DESCARTES

(1596-1650)

"I had long since remarked that in matters of conduct it is necessary sometimes to follow opinions known to be uncertain, as if they were not subject to doubt; but, because now I was desirous to devote myself to the search after truth, I considered that I must do just the contrary, and reject as absolutely false everything concerning which I could imagine the least doubt to exist."

Many historians of philosophy agree that modern philosophy began with Descartes. In his emphasis on the usefulness of mathematics, in his reliance on individual intellectual autonomy, he established the rational skepticism that became the prevailing temperament of thinkers after his time.

As a young student he excelled because he had faith in the knowledge transmitted to him in the classroom. But his true brilliance emerged as his growing doubt about the worth of the knowledge he had mastered led him to the liberating experience of embracing the power of his own mind.

In *Discourse on Method* Descartes offers a highly readable account of the evolution of his own thought processes and, by extension, provides a preview of the intellectual development which was to follow in Europe and America.

DISCOURSE ON METHOD

RENÉ DESCARTES

I-The Aim of the Discourse

Good sense or reason must be better distributed than anything else in the world, for no man desires more of it than he already has. This shows that reason is by nature equal in all men. If there is diversity of opinion, this arises from the fact that we conduct our thought by different ways and consider not the same things. It does not suffice that the understanding be good—it must be well applied.

My mind is no better than another's, but I have been lucky enough to chance on certain ways, which have led me to a certain method by means of which it seems to me that I may by degrees augment my knowledge to the modest measure of my intellect and my length of days. I shall be very glad to make plain in this Discourse the paths I have followed, and to picture my life so that all may judge of it, and by the setting forth of their opinions may furnish me with yet other means of improvement.

It is my design not to teach the method which each man ought to follow for the right guidance of his reason, but only to show in what manner I have tried to conduct my own.

I have been nourished on letters from my infancy, but as soon as I had finished the customary course of study, I found myself hampered by so many doubts and errors that I seemed to have reaped no benefits, except that I had observed more and more of my ignorance. Yet I was at one of the most celebrated schools in Europe, and I was not held inferior to my fellow-students, some of whom were destined to take the place of our masters; nor did our age seem less fruitful of good wits than any which had gone before.

Though I did not cease to esteem the studies of the schools, I began to think that I had given enough time to languages, enough also to ancient books, their stories and their fables; for when a man spends too much time in travelling abroad, he becomes a stranger in his own country; and so, when he is too curious concerning what went on in past ages, he is apt to remain ignorant of what is taking place in his own day. I set a high price on eloquence, and I was in love with poetry; I rejoiced in mathematics, but knew nothing of its true use.

I revered our theology, but, since the way to heaven lies open to the ignorant no less than to the learned, and the revealed truths which lead thither are beyond our intelligence, I did not dare to submit them to my feeble reasonings.

In philosophy there is no truth which is not disputed and which, consequently, is not doubtful; the other sciences all borrow their principles from philosophy.

Therefore, I entirely gave up the study of letters and employed the rest of my youth in travelling, being resolved to seek no other science than that which I might find within myself, or in the great Book of the World.

Here the best lesson that I learnt was not to believe too firmly anything of which I had learnt merely by example and custom; and thus little by little was delivered from many errors which are liable to obscure the light of nature and to diminish our capacity of hearing reason. Finally, I resolved one day to study myself in the same way, and in this it seems to me I succeeded much better than if I had never departed from either my country or my books.

II-The Intellectual Crisis

Being in Germany, on my way to rejoin the army after the coronation of the Emperor [Ferdinand II], I was lying at an inn where, in default of other conversation, I was at liberty to entertain my own thoughts. Of these, one of the first was that often there is less perfection in works which are composite than in those which issue from a single hand. Such was the case with buildings, cities, states; for a people which has made its laws from time to time to meet particular occasions will enjoy a less perfect polity than a people which from the beginning has observed the constitution of a farsighted legislator. This is very certain, that the estate of true religion, which God alone has ordained, must be incomparably better guided than any other.

And again, I considered that as, during our childhood, we had been governed by our appetites and our tutors, which are often at variance, which neither of them perhaps always gave us the best counsel, it is almost impossible that our judgments should be so pure and so solid as they would have been if we had had the perfect use of our reason from the time of our birth and had never been guided by anything else.

Hence, as regarded the opinions that I had received into my belief, I thought that, as a private person may pull down his own house to build a finer, so I could not do better than remove them therefrom in order to replace them by sounder, or, after I should have adjusted them to the level of reason, to establish the same once more.

When I was younger I had studied logic, analytical geometry and algebra. Of these, I found that logic served rather for explaining things we already know; while of geometry and algebra, the former is so tied to the consideration of figures that it cannot exercise the understanding without wearying the imagination, and the latter is so bound down to certain rules and ciphers that it has been made a confused and obscure art which hampers the mind instead of a science which cultivates it. And as a state is better governed which has but few laws, and those strictly observed, I believed that I should find sufficient these four precepts:

The first was never to accept anything as true when I did not recognize it clearly to be so—that is to say, carefully to avoid precipitation and prejudice, but to include in my opinions nothing beyond that which should present itself so clearly and distinctly to my mind that I might have no occasion to doubt it.

The second was to divide up the difficulties which I should examine into as many parts as possible, and as should be required for their better resolution.

The third was to conduct my thoughts in order, by beginning with the simplest objects, so as to mount little by little, by stages, to the most complex knowledge, even supposing an order among things which did not naturally stand in an order of antecedent and consequent.

And the last was to make everywhere enumerations so complete, and surveys so wide, that I should be sure of omitting nothing.

Exact observation of these precepts gave me such facility in unravelling the questions comprehended in geometrical analysis and in algebra, that in two or three months not only did I find my way through many which I had formerly accounted too hard for me, but towards the end, I seemed to be able to determine, in those which were new to me, by what means and to what extent it was possible to resolve them.

And so I promised myself that I would apply my system with equal success to the difficulties of other sciences; but since their principles must all be borrowed from philosophy, in which I found no certain principles of its own, I thought that before all else I must try to establish some therein. By way of preparation (for I was then but twenty-three years old) I must root up from my mind my previous bad opinion of it, and must practise my method in order that I might be confirmed in it.

III-A Rule of Life

Meanwhile I must have a rule of life as a shelter while my new house was in building, and this consisted of three or four maxims.

The first was to conform myself to the laws and customs of my country and to hold to the religion in which, by God's grace, I had been brought up; guiding myself, for the rest, by the least extreme opinions of the most intelligent. Among extremes I counted all promises by which a man curtails anything of his liberty; for I should have deemed it a grave fault against good sense if, because I approved something in a given moment, I had bound myself to accept it as good for ever after.

My second maxim was to follow resolutely even doubtful opinions when sure opinions were not available, just as the traveller, lost in some forest, had better walk straight forward, though in a chance direction; for thus he will arrive, if not precisely where he desires to be, at least at a better place than the middle of a forest.

My third maxim was to endeavour always to conquer myself rather than fortune, and to change my desires rather than the order of the world, and in general to bring myself to believe that there is nothing wholly in our power except our thoughts. And I believe that herein lay the secret of those philosophers who, in the days of old, could withdraw from the domination of fortune and, despite pain and poverty, challenge the felicity of their gods.

Finally, after looking out upon the divers occupations of men, I pondered that I could do no better than persevere in that which I had chosen—so deep was my content in discovering every day by its means truths which seemed to me important, yet were unknown to the world.

Having thus made myself sure of these maxims, and having set them apart together with the verities of faith, I judged that for the rest of my opinions I might set freely to work to divest myself of them. For nine years, therefore, I went up and down the world a spectator rather than an actor. These nine years slipped away before I had begun to seek for the foundations of any philosophy more certain, nor perhaps should I have dared to undertake the quest had it not been put about that I had already succeeded.

IV-'I Think, Therefore I Am'

I had long since remarked that in matters of conduct it is necessary sometimes to follow opinions known to be uncertain, as if they were not subject to doubt; but, because now I was desirous to devote myself to the search after truth, I considered that I must do just the contrary, and reject as absolutely false everything concerning which I could imagine the least doubt to exist.

Thus, because our senses sometimes deceive us, I would suppose that nothing is such as they make us to imagine it; and because I was as likely to err as another in reasoning, I rejected as false all the reasons which I had formerly accepted as demonstrative; and finally, considering that all the thoughts we have when awake can come to us also when we sleep without any of them being true, I resolved to feign that everything which had ever entered my mind was no more truth than the illusion of my dreams.

But I observed that, while I was thus resolved to feign that everything was false, I who thought must of necessity be somewhat; and remarking this truth—*I think, therefore I am*—was so firm and so assured that all the most extravagant suppositions of the sceptics were unable to shake it, I judged that I could unhesitatingly accept it as the first principle of the philosophy I was seeking. I could feign that there was no world, I could not feign that I did not exist. And I judged that I might take it as a general rule that the things which we conceive very clearly and very distinctly are all true, and that the only difficulty lies in the way of discerning which those things are that we conceive distinctly.

After this, reflecting upon the fact that I doubted, and that consequently my being was not quite perfected (for I saw that to *know* is a greater perfection than to *doubt*), I bethought me to inquire whence I had learnt to think of something more perfect than myself; and it was clear to me that this must come from some nature which was in fact more perfect. For other things I could regard as dependencies of my nature if they were real, and if they were not real they might proceed from nothing—that is to say, they might exist in me by way of defect.

But it could not be the same with the idea of a being more perfect than my own; for to derive it from nothing was manifestly impossible; and because it is no less repugnant that the more perfect should follow and depend upon the less perfect than that something should come forth out of nothing. I could not derive it from myself.

It remained, then, to conclude that it was put into me by a nature truly more perfect than was I and possessing in itself all the perfections of what I could form an idea—in a word, by God. To which I added that, since I knew some perfections which I did not possess, I was not the only being who existed, but that there must of necessity be some other being, more perfect, on whom I depended, and from whom I had acquired all that I possessed; for if I had existed alone and independent of all other, so that I had of myself all this little whereby I participated in the Perfect Being. I should have been able to have in myself all those other qualities which I knew myself to lack, and so to be infinite, eternal, immutable, omniscient, almighty—in fine, to possess all the perfections which I could observe in God.

Proposing to myself the geometer's subject matter, and then turning again to examine my idea of a Perfect Being, I found that existence was comprehended in that idea just as in the idea of a triangle is comprehended the notion that the sum of its angles is equal to two right angles; and that consequently it is as certain that God, this Perfect Being is or exists, as any geometrical demonstration could be.

That there are many who persuade themselves that there is a difficulty in knowing Him is due to the scholastic maxim that there is nothing in the understanding which has not first been in the senses; where the ideas of God and the soul have never been.

Than the existence of God all other things, even those which it seems to a man extravagant to doubt, such as his having a body, are less certain. Nor is there any reason sufficient to remove such doubt but such as presupposes the existence of God. From His existence it follows that our ideas or notions, being real things, and coming from God, cannot but be true in so far as they are clear and distinct. In so far as they contain falsity, they are confused and obscure, there is in them an element of mere negation (*elles participent du neant*); that is to say, they are thus confused in us because we ourselves are not all perfect. And it is evident that falsity or imperfection can no more come forth from God than can perfection proceed from nothingness. But, did we not know that all which is in us of the real and the true comes from a perfect and infinite being, however clear and distinct our ideas might be, we should have no reason for assurance that they possessed the final perfection—truth.

Reason instructs us that all our ideas must have some foundation of truth, for it could not be that the All-Perfect and the All-True should otherwise have put them into us; and because our reasonings are never so evident or so complete when we sleep as when we wake, although sometimes during sleep our imagination may be more vivid and positive, it also instructs us that such truth as our thoughts have will be in our waking thoughts rather than in our dreams.

V-Why I do not Publish 'The World'

I have always remained firm in my resolve to assume no other principle than that which I have used to demonstrate the existence of God and of the soul, and to receive nothing which did not seem to me clearer and more certain than the demonstrations of the philosophers had seemed before; yet not only have I found means of satisfying myself with regard to the principal difficulties which are usually treated of in philosophy, but also I have remarked certain laws which God has so established in nature, and of which He has implanted such notions in our souls, that we cannot doubt that they are observed in all which happens in the world.

The principal truths which flow from these I have tried to unfold in a treatise (On the World, or on Light), which certain considerations prevent me from publishing. This I concluded three years ago, and had begun to revise it for the printer, when I learnt that certain persons to whom I defer had disapproved an opinion on physics published a short time before by a certain person (Galileo, condemned by the Roman Inquisition in 1633), in which opinion I had noticed nothing prejudicial to religion; and this made me fear that there might be some among my opinions in which I was mistaken.

I now believe that I ought to continue to write all the things which I judge of importance, but ought in no wise to consent to their publication during my life. For my experience of the objections which might be made forbids me to hope for any profit from them. I have tried both friends and enemies, yet it has seldom happened that they have offered any objection which I had not in some measure foreseen; so that I have never, I may say, found a critic who did not seem to be either less rigorous or less fair-minded than myself.

Whereupon I gladly take this opportunity to beg those who shall come after us never to believe that the things which they are told come from me unless I have divulged them myself; and I am in nowise astonished at the extravagances attributed to those old philosophers whose writings have not come down to us. They were the greatest minds of their time, but have been ill reported.

Why, I am sure that the most devoted of those who now follow Aristotle would esteem themselves happy if they had as much knowledge of nature as he had, even on the condition that they should never have more! They are like ivy, which never mounts higher than the trees which support it, and which even comes down again after it has attained their summit. So at least, it seems to me, do they who, not content with knowing all that is explained by their author, would find in him the solution also of many difficulties of which he says nothing, and of which, perhaps, he never thought.

Yet their method of philosophising is very convenient for those who have but middling minds, for the obscurity of the distinctions and principles which they employ enables them to speak of all things as boldly as if they had knowledge of them, and sustain all they have to say against the most subtle and skilful without there being any means of convincing them; wherein they seem to me like a blind man who, in order to fight on equal terms with a man who has his sight, invites him into the depths of a cavern.

And I may say that it is to their interest that I should abstain from publishing the principles of the philosophy which I employ, for so simple and so evident are they that to publish them would be like opening windows into their caverns and letting in the day. But if they prefer acquaintance with a little truth, and desire to follow a plan like mine, there is no need for me to say to them any more in this discourse than I have already said.

For if they are capable of passing beyond what I have done, much rather will they be able to discover for themselves whatever I believe myself to have found out; besides which, the practice which they will acquire in seeking out easy things and thence passing to others which are more difficult, will stead them better than all my instructions.

But if some of the matters spoken about at the beginning of the Dioptrics and the Meteors [published with the Discourse on Method] should at first give offence because I have called them 'suppositions,' and have shown no desire to prove them, let the reader have patience to read the whole attentively, and I have hope that he will be satisfied.

The time remaining to me I have resolved to employ in trying to acquire some knowledge of nature, such that we may be able to draw from it more certain rules for medicine than those which we possess. And I hereby declare that I shall always hold myself more obliged to those by whose favour I enjoy my leisure undisturbed than I should be to any who should offer me the most esteemed employments in the world.

BENEDICT SPINOZA

(1632-1677)

"All the objects pursued by the multitude not only bring no remedy that tends to preserve our being, but even act as hindrances, causing the death not seldom of those who possess them, and always of those who are possessed by them."

Born Baruch Spinoza, this disciple of the emerging scientific rationalism, was excommunicated from his Amsterdam synagogue for heresy. Isolated from his Jewish congregation, Spinoza took the Latin form of his given name and is known to history as Benedict (Blessed). Despite what were then, and in some quarters still are, his radical views on theology, metaphysics, ethics, and politics, Spinoza acquired a small and devoted following in his lifetime. The challenging content of his ideas kept much of his work, notably his masterpiece, *The Ethics*, from being published while he was alive. *The Ethics* is a demanding, highly technical investigation into human psychology and behavior. The few pages included here are from a shorter work, "On the Improvement of the Understanding." In it Spinoza makes clear the perils of common desires and ambitions and suggests an alternative approach to life that in his view is both more rewarding and more ethical.

ON THE IMPROVEMENT OF THE UNDERSTANDING.

BENEDICT SPINOZA

After experience had taught me that all the usual surroundings of social life are vain and futile; seeing that none of the objects of my fears contained in themselves anything either good or bad, except in so far as the mind is affected by them, I finally resolved to inquire whether there might be some real good having power to communicate itself, which would affect the mind singly, to the exclusion of all else: whether, in fact, there might be anything of which the discovery and attainment would enable me to enjoy continuous, supreme, and unending happiness. I say "I *finally* resolved," for at first sight it seemed unwise willingly to lose hold on what was sure for the sake of something then uncertain. I could see the benefits which are acquired through fame and riches, and that I should be obliged to abandon the quest for such objects, if I seriously devoted myself to the search for something different and new. I perceived that if true happiness chanced to be placed in the former I should necessarily miss it; while if, on the other hand, it were not so placed, and I gave them my whole attention, I should equally fail.

I therefore debated whether it would not be possible to arrive at the new principle, or at any rate at a certainty concerning its existence, without changing the conduct and usual plan of my life; with this end in view I made many efforts, but in vain. For the ordinary surroundings of life which are esteemed by men (as their actions testify) to be the highest good, may be classed under the three heads—Riches, Fame, and the Pleasures of Sense: with these three the mind is so absorbed that it has little power to reflect on any different good. By sensual pleasure the mind is enthralled to the extent of quiescence, as if the supreme good were actually attained, so that it is quite incapable of thinking of any other object; when such pleasure has been gratified it is followed by extreme melancholy, whereby the mind, though not enthralled, is disturbed and dulled.

The pursuit of honours and riches is likewise very absorbing, especially if such objects be sought simply for their own sake, inasmuch as they are then supposed to constitute the highest good. In the case of fame the mind is still more absorbed, for fame is conceived as always good for its own sake, and as the ultimate end to which all actions are directed. Further, the attainment of riches and fame is not followed as in the case of sensual pleasures by repentance, but, the more we acquire, the greater is our delight, and, consequently, the more are we incited to increase both the one and the other; on the other hand, if our hopes happen to be frustrated we are plunged into the deepest sadness. Fame has the further drawback that it compels its votaries to order their lives according to the opinions of their fellow-men, shunning what they usually shun, and seeking what they usually seek.

When I saw that all these ordinary objects of desire would be obstacles in the way of a search for something different and new—nay, that they were so opposed thereto, that either they or it would have to be abandoned, I was forced to inquire which would prove the most useful to me: for, as I say, I seemed to be willingly losing hold on a sure good for the sake of something uncertain. However, after I had reflected on the matter, I came in the first place to the conclusion that by abandoning the ordinary objects of pursuit, and betaking myself to a new quest, I should be leaving a good, uncertain by reason of its own nature, as may be gathered from what has been said, for the sake of a good not uncertain in its nature (for I sought for a fixed good), but only in the possibility of its attainment.

Further reflection convinced me, that if I could really get to the root of the matter I should be leaving certain evils for a certain good. I thus perceived that I was in a state of great peril, and I compelled myself to seek with all my strength for a remedy, however uncertain it might be;

as a sick man struggling with a deadly disease, when he sees that death will surely be upon him unless a remedy be found, is compelled to seek such a remedy with all his strength, inasmuch as his whole hope lies therein. All the objects pursued by the multitude not only bring no remedy that tends to preserve our being, but even act as hindrances, causing the death not seldom of those who possess them, and always of those who are possessed by them. There are many examples of men who have suffered persecution even to death for the sake of their riches, and of men who in pursuit of wealth have exposed themselves to so many dangers, that they have paid away their life as a penalty for their folly. Examples are no less numerous of men, who have endured the utmost wretchedness for the sake of gaining or preserving their reputation. Lastly, there are innumerable cases of men, who have hastened their death through over-indulgence in sensual pleasure. All these evils seem to have arisen from the fact, that happiness or unhappiness is made wholly to depend on the quality of the object which we love. When a thing is not loved, no quarrels will arise concerning it—no sadness will be felt if it perishes—no envy if it is possessed by another—no fear, no hatred, in short no disturbances of the mind. All these arise from the love of what is perishable, such as the objects already mentioned. But love towards a thing eternal and infinite feeds the mind wholly with joy, and is itself unmingled with any sadness, wherefore it is greatly to be desired and sought for with all our strength. Yet it was not at random that I used the words, "If I could go to the root of the matter," for, though what I have urged was perfectly clear to my mind, I could not forthwith lay aside all love of riches, sensual enjoyment, and fame. One thing was evident, namely, that while my mind was employed with these thoughts it turned away from its former objects of desire, and seriously considered the search for a new principle; this state of things was a great comfort to me, for I perceived that the evils were not such as to resist all remedies. Although these intervals were at first rare, and of very short duration, yet afterwards, as the true good became more and more discernible to me, they became more frequent and more lasting; especially after I had recognized that the acquisition of wealth, sensual pleasure, or fame, is only a hindrance, so long as they are sought as ends not as means; if they be sought as means, they will be under restraint, and, far from being hindrances, will further not a little the end for which they are sought, as I will show in due time.

    I will here only briefly state what I mean by true good, and also what is the nature of the highest good. In order that this may be rightly understood, we must bear in mind that the terms good and evil are only applied relatively, so that the same thing may be called both good and bad, according to the relations in view, in the same way as it may be called perfect or imperfect. Nothing regarded in its own nature can be called perfect or imperfect; especially when we are aware that all things which come to pass, come to pass according to the eternal order and fixed laws of nature. However, human weakness cannot attain to this order in its own thoughts, but meanwhile man conceives a human character much more stable than his own, and sees that there is no reason why he should not himself acquire such a character. Thus he is led to seek for means which will bring him to this pitch of perfection, and calls everything which will serve as such means a true good. The chief good is that he should arrive, together with other individuals if possible, at the possession of the aforesaid character. What that character is we shall show in due time, namely, that it is the knowledge of the union existing between the mind and the whole of nature. This, then, is the end for which I strive, to attain to such a character myself, and to endeavour that many should attain to it with me. In other words, it is part of my happiness to lend a helping hand, that many others may understand even as I do, so that their understanding and desire may entirely agree with my own. In order to bring this about, it is necessary to understand as much of nature as will enable us to attain to the aforesaid character, and also to form a social order such as is most conducive to the attainment of this character by the greatest number with the least difficulty and danger. We must seek the assistance of Moral Philosophy and the Theory of Education; further, as health is no insignificant means for attaining our end, we must also include the whole science of Medicine, and, as many difficult things are by contrivance rendered easy, and we can in this way gain much time and convenience, the science of Mechanics must in no way be despised. But, before all things, a means must be devised for improving the understanding and purifying it, as far as may be at the outset, so that it may apprehend things without error, and in the best possible way.

Thus it is apparent to everyone that I wish to direct all sciences to one end and aim, so that we may attain to the supreme human perfection which we have named; and, therefore, whatsoever in the sciences does not serve to promote our object will have to be rejected as useless. To sum up the matter in a word, all our actions and thoughts must be directed to this one end. Yet, as it is necessary that while we are endeavouring to attain our purpose, and bring the understanding into the right path, we should carry on our life, we are compelled first of all to lay down certain rules of life as provisionally good, to wit the following:—

I. To speak in a manner intelligible to the multitude, and to comply with every general custom that does not hinder the attainment of our purpose. For we can gain from the multitude no small advantages, provided that we strive to accommodate ourselves to its understanding as far as possible: moreover, we shall in this way gain a friendly audience for the reception of the truth.

II. To indulge ourselves with pleasures only in so far as they are necessary for preserving health.

III. Lastly, to endeavour to obtain only sufficient money or other commodities to enable us to preserve our life and health, and to follow such general customs as are consistent with our purpose.

JOHN LOCKE

(1632-1704)

"Perception, then, is the first operation of intellectual faculties, and the inlet of all knowledge into our minds."

John Locke was born in England in 1632. Noted not just as a philosopher, but as an Oxford Don, scientist, medical doctor, and economist, he is truly one of the most eclectic thinkers in the Western tradition. Locke, in direct contrast to Thomas Hobbes, believed in the essential goodness of man. According to Locke, it is society that corrupts man. In advocating certain inalienable rights inherent to all men, Locke would influence the budding Constitutional Monarchy in England and eventually the revolutionary movements in America and France.

Locke's *An Essay Concerning Human Understanding* attempts to determine the limits of what mankind can know. Locke felt that man enters the world as a blank slate, what he referred to as a *tabula rasa*. This empirical view of philosophy holds that we have no knowledge prior to experience. We can know only the appearances and not the underlying qualities that produce these experiences.

An Essay Concerning Human Understanding stands as a cornerstone of empirical philosophy. To a large extent the direction of empirical philosophy was in response to Locke's essay. Berkeley, Hume, and eventually Kant, all make direct references to Locke in their attempts to address the notion of the limits of human understanding.

AN ESSAY CONCERNING HUMAN UNDERSTANDING

JOHN LOCKE

I-The Nature of Simple Ideas

'Idea' being that term which, I think, serves best to stand for whatsoever is the object of the understanding, I have used it to express whatever is meant by phantasm, notion, species, or whatever it is the mind can be, employed about in thinking. Let us, then, suppose the mind to be, as we say, white paper void of all characters—without any ideas. Whence comes it by that vast store which the busy and boundless fancy of man has painted on it with an almost endless variety? To this, I answer in one word-experience; in that all our knowledge is founded, and from that it ultimately derives itself.

Let anyone examine his own thoughts and thoroughly search his understanding, and then let him tell me whether of all the original ideas he has there are any other than of the objects of his senses, or of the observations of his mind considered as objects of his reflection.

Though the qualities that affect our senses are, in the things themselves, so united and blended that there is no separation, no distance between them, yet it is plain the ideas they produce in the mind enter by the senses simple and unmixed. For though the sight and touch often take in from the same object at the same time different ideas, yet the simple ideas thus united in the same subject are as perfectly distinct as those that come in by different senses; the coldness and hardness which a man feels in a piece of ice being as distinct ideas in the mind as the smell and whiteness of a lily, and each of them being in itself uncompounded contains nothing but one uniform appearance, or conception, in the mind, and is not distinguishable into different ideas.

When the understanding is once stored with these simple ideas, it has the power to repeat, compare and unite them even to an almost infinite variety, and so can make at will new complex ideas. But it is not in the power of any most exalted wit or enlarged understanding, by any quickness or variety of thought, to invent or frame one new simple idea in the mind, nor to destroy those that are there. I would have anyone try to fancy any taste which had never affected his palate, or frame the idea of a scent he had never smelt; and when he can do this, I will also conclude that a blind man hath ideas of colours and a deaf man true, distinct notions of sound.

There are some ideas which have admittance only through one sense which is peculiarly adapted to receive them. Thus, light and colours come in only by the eye, all kinds of noises by the ear, the tastes and smells by the nose and palate. The most considerable of those belonging to the touch are heat, cold and solidity—which is the idea that belongs to the body, whereby we conceive it to fill space.

Simple ideas of divers senses are the ideas of space or extension, figure, rest and motion, for these make perceivable impressions on the eyes and touch, and we can receive and convey into our minds the ideas of the extension, figure, motion and rest of bodies by seeing and feeling.

The mind, receiving the ideas mentioned in the foregoing from without, when it turns its view inward upon itself and observes its own actions about those ideas it has, takes from thence other ideas which are as capable to be the objects of its contemplation as any of those it received from foreign things.

The two great and principal actions of the mind which are most frequently considered, and which are so frequent that everyone that pleases may take notice of them in himself, are these two: perception or thinking, and volition or will. The power of thinking is called the understanding, and the power of volition is called the will. And these two powers or abilities in the mind are denominated faculties. Modes of these simple ideas of reflection are rememberance, discerning, reasoning, judging, knowledge, faith.

It has, further, pleased our wise Creator to annex to several objects and to the ideas which we receive from them, as also to several of our thoughts, a concomitant pleasure, and that in several objects to several degrees, that those faculties which He has endowed us with might not remain wholly unemployed by us. Pain has the same efficacy and use to set us on work that pleasure had, we being as ready to employ our faculties to avoid that as to pursue this.

Existence and unity are two other ideas that are suggested to the understanding by every object without and every idea within. Power is another of those simple ideas which we receive from sensation and reflection; and, besides these, there is succession.

Nor let anyone think these too narrow bounds for the capacious mind of man to expatiate in, which takes its flight farther than the stars and cannot be confined by the limits of the world, that extends its thoughts often even beyond the utmost expansion of matter and makes excursions into that incomprehensible inane. Nor will it be so strange to think these few simple ideas sufficient to employ the quickest thought or largest capacity if we consider how many words may be made out of the various composition of twenty-four letters; or if, going one step farther, we will but reflect on the variety of combinations that may be made with barely one of the above mentioned ideas—viz. number, whose stock is inexhaustible. And what a large and immense field doth extension alone afford the mathematicians!

II-Of Idea-Producing Qualities

The power to produce any idea in our mind I call quality of the subject wherein the power is. Qualities are, first, such as are utterly inseparable from the body in what state soever it be. These I call original or primary qualities, which I think we may observe to produce simple ideas in us—viz. solidity, extension, figure, motion or rest, and number.

Secondly, such qualities which in truth are nothing in the objects themselves, but powers to produce various sensations in us by their primary qualities—i.e. by the bulk, figure, texture and motion of their insensible parts. These secondary qualities are colours, sounds, tastes, etc. From whence it is easy to draw this observation: that the ideas of primary qualities of bodies are resemblances of them, but the ideas produced in us by the secondary qualities have no resemblance in them at all.

If anyone will consider that the same fire that at one distance produces in us the sensation of warmth does, at a nearer approach, produce in us the far different sensation of pain, let him bethink himself what reason he has to say that this idea of warmth, which was produced in him by the fire, is actually in the fire; and his idea of pain, which the same fire produced in him in the same way, is not in the fire. The particular bulk, number, figure and motion of the parts of fire or snow are really in them, whether anyone's senses perceive them or not; and, therefore, they may be called real qualities, because they really exist in those bodies. But light, heat, whiteness, or coldness are no more really in them than sickness or pain is in man. Take away the sensation of them; let not the eyes see light or colours, nor the ears hear sounds; let the palate not taste, nor the nose smell; and all colours, tastes, odours and sounds vanish and are reduced to their causes—i.e. bulk, figure and motion of parts.

III-Various Faculties of the Mind

What perception is everyone will know better by reflecting on what he does himself when he sees, hears, feels, tastes, smells or thinks, than by any discourse of mine.

We ought further to consider concerning perceptions, that the ideas we receive by sensation are often in grown people altered by the judgement without our taking any notice of it.

When we set before our eyes a round globe of uniform colour— e.g. gold, alabaster or jet—the idea thereby imprinted in our mind is of a flat circle variously shadowed with several degrees of light and brightness coming to our eyes.

But we, having by use been accustomed to perceive what kind of appearances convex bodies are wont to make in us, what alterations are made in the reflections of light by the difference of the sensible figures of bodies, the judgement presently, by an habitual custom, alters the appearances into their causes; so that from that which is truly a variety of shadow or colour collecting the figure, it makes it pass for a mark of figure, and frames to itself the perception of a convex figure and a uniform colour, when the idea we receive from thence is only a plane variously coloured, as is evident in painting.

Perception, then, is the first operation of our intellectual faculties, and the inlet of all knowledge into our minds.

The next faculty of the mind whereby it makes a further progress towards knowledge is that which I call retention, or the keeping of those simple ideas which from sensation or reflection it hath received. This is done, first, by keeping the idea which is brought into it for some time actually in view, which is called contemplation. The other way of retention is the power to revive again in our minds those ideas which after imprinting have disappeared, or have been, as it were, laid aside out of sight; and thus we do when we conceive heat or light, yellow or sweet, the object being removed. This is memory, the store-house of our ideas.

Another faculty we may take notice of in our minds is that of discerning and distinguishing between the several ideas it has. It is not enough to have a confused perception of something in general. Unless the mind had a distinct perception of different objects and their qualities, it would be capable of very little knowledge, even though the bodies that affect us were as busy about us as they are now, and though the mind were continually employed in thinking.

On this faculty of distinguishing one thing from another depend the evidence and certainty of several even very general propositions which have passed for innate truths, because men, overlooking the true cause why those proportions find universal assent, impute it wholly to native uniform impressions; whereas it, in truth, depends upon this clear discerning faculty of the mind, whereby it perceives two ideas to be the same or to be different.

The comparing of ideas one with another is the operation of the mind upon which depends all that large tribe of ideas comprehended under relations. The next operation is composition, whereby the mind puts together several simple ideas and combines them into complex ones.

The use of words being to stand as outward marks of our internal ideas, and those ideas being taken from particular things, if every particular idea that we take in should have a distinct name, names must be endless. To prevent this, the mind makes the particular ideas received from particular objects to become general, which is done by considering them as they are in the mind, and such appearances separate from all other existences and from the circumstances of real existence, as time, place, or any other concomitant ideas.

This is called abstraction, whereby ideas taken from particular being become general representatives of all of the same kind. Thus, the same colour being observed to-day in chalk or snow which the mind yesterday received from milk, it considers that that appearance alone makes it a representative of all of that kind; and having given it the name 'whiteness,' it by that sound signifies the same quality wheresoever imagined or met with; and thus universals, whether ideas or terms, are made.

As the mind is wholly passive in the reception of all its simple ideas, so it exerts several acts of its own, whereby, out of its simple ideas, as the materials and foundations of the rest the others are framed. And I believe we shall find, if we observe the originals of our notions, that even the most abstruse ideas, how remote soever they may seen from sense, or from any operation of our minds, are yet only such as the understanding frames to itself, by repeating and joining together ideas that it had either from objects of sense or from its own operations about them; so that even those large and abstract ideas are derived from sensation or reflection, being no other than what the mind, by the ordinary use of its own faculties employed about ideas received from objects of sense, or from the operations it observes in itself about them, may and does attain. This may be shown in our ideas of space, time and infinity, and some others that seem the most remote from these originals.

IV-Our Knowledge of the Existence of Other Things

It is the actual receiving of ideas from without that gives us notice of the existence of other things, and makes us know that something does exist at that time without us which causes that idea in us, though perhaps we neither know nor consider how it does it. And this, though not so certain as our own intuitive knowledge, or as the deductions of our reason employed about the clear abstract ideas of our own minds, yet deserves the name of knowledge.

It is plain that those perceptions are produced by exterior causes affecting our senses for the following reasons:

Because those that lack the physical organs of any sense never can have the ideas belonging to that sense produced in their minds.

Because sometimes I find I cannot avoid having those ideas produced in my mind; for as when my eyes are shut, or the windows fast, I can at pleasure recall to my mind the ideas of light or the sun which former sensations have lodged in my memory; so I can at pleasure lay by that idea and take into my view that of a rose or taste of sugar. But if I turn my eyes at noon towards the sun, I cannot avoid the ideas which the light or sun produces in me. There is nobody who does not perceive the difference in himself contemplating the sun as he has an idea of it in his memory and actually looking upon it, of which two his perception is so distinct that few of his ideas are more distinguishable one from another; and, therefore, he has certain knowledge that they are not both memory or the action of his mind and fancies only within him, but that actual seeing has a cause without.

Add to this that many of those ideas are produced with pain, which afterwards we remember without the least offence.

Lastly, our senses bear witness to the truth of each other's report concerning the existence of sensible things without us and around us.

JEAN JACQUES ROUSSEAU

(1712-1788)

"Man is born free, and yet is everywhere in fetters."

Jean Jacques Rousseau was born in Geneva, Switzerland. Following a troubled youth, Rousseau took up residence in Paris. After winning an important essay contest in which he railed against the progress of the sciences, Rousseau became a well known writer and philosopher. In contrast to the mainstream of the Enlightenment, Rousseau was a proponent of emotion and nature as truer and more reliable than reason alone. Nature, according to Rousseau, held the key to leading a good life. Only a natural life could allow mankind to live in peace and harmony with his fellow men, and with himself. Rousseau's works would have a profound influence on philosophy, the arts, and on political theory.

The Social Contract is perhaps Rousseau's most enduring and influential work. Like Hobbes, Rousseau recognized the need for mankind to create political units. Unlike Hobbes, Rousseau saw mankind as essentially good. But mankind has strayed so far from nature that he cannot return to its unspoiled simplicity. He must now form social contracts to ensure his freedom. The controversy surrounding *The Social Contract* is substantial. While Rousseau seems to imply that the social contract can only come about through the agreement of the people, he leaves us somewhat in doubt as to how the contract is to be formed. He speaks of a General Will of the people. But how is the General Will to be discerned?

Because of the vagueness of Rousseau's *The Social Contract*, it has alternatively been cited by advocates of democratic states, dictatorships, and virtually every other type of government, as supporting their particular theory. Indeed, Karl Marx used portions of *The Social Contract* in his *Communist Manifesto*. Rousseau died a year before the onset of the French Revolution, but his writings, especially *The Social Contract,* would have a substantial impact on the revolution.

THE SOCIAL CONTRACT

JEAN JACQUES ROUSSEAU

I-The Terms of the Compact

My object is to discover whether in civil polity there is any legitimate and definite canon of government, taking men as they are and laws as they might be. In this inquiry I shall uniformly try to reconcile that which is permitted by right with that which is prescribed by interest so as to avoid the clash of justice with utility.

Man is born free, and yet is everywhere in fetters. He is governed, obliged to obey laws. What is it that legitimises this subjection to government? I think I can solve the problem.

It is not merely a matter of force; force is only the power of the strongest and must yield when a greater strength arises; there is here no question of right, but simply of might. But social order is a sacred right that serves as a base to all others. This right, however, does not come from nature; it is founded upon conventions.

The explanation of social order is not to be found in the family tie, since when a child grows up it escapes from tutelage; the parent's right to exercise authority is only temporary. Nor can government be based on servitude. An individual man may sell his liberty to another for sustenance; but a nation cannot sell its liberty—it does not receive sustenance from its ruler but, on the contrary, sustains him. The gift is a civil act which presupposes a public deliberation. Before, then, we examine the act by which a people chooses a king, it would be well to examine the act by which a people becomes a people.

Let it be assumed that the obstacles which prejudice the conversation of man in the state of nature have prevailed by their resistance over the forces which each individual is able to employ to keep himself in that state. The primitive condition can then no longer exist; mankind must change it or perish.

The problem with which men are confronted in these circumstances may be stated as follows: 'To find a form of association that defends and protects with all the common force the person and property of each partner, and by which each partner, uniting himself with all the rest, nevertheless obeys only himself, and remains as free as heretofore.' To this problem the social contract affords a solution.

The essence of the pact is the total and unreserved alienation by each partner of all his rights to the community as a whole. No individual can retain any rights that are not possessed equally by all other individuals without the compact being thereby violated. Again, each partner, by yielding his rights to the community, yields them to no individual, and thus in his relations with individuals he regains all the rights he has sacrificed.

The compact, therefore, may be reduced to the following terms: 'Each of us places in common his person and all his power under the supreme direction of the general will, and we receive each member as an indivisible part of the whole.'

By this act is created a moral and collective body, composed of as many members as the society has voices, receiving from this same act its unity, its common 'I,' its life and its will. This body is the republic, called by its members the state when passive, the sovereign when active. The partners are collectively called the people; they are citizens, as participants in the sovereign authority, and subjects, as under obligations to the laws of the state.

By passing through the compact, from the state of nature to the civil state man substitutes justice for instinct in his conduct and gives to his actions a morality of which they were formerly devoid. What man loses by the contract is his natural liberty and an illimitable right to all that tempts him and that he can obtain; what he gains is civil liberty and a right of secure property in all that he possesses.

I shall conclude this chapter with a remark which should serve as a basis for the whole social system. It is that in place of destroying natural liberty, the fundamental pact substitutes a moral and legitimate equality for the natural physical inequality between men, and that, while men may be unequal in strength and talent, they are all made equal by convention and right.

II-The Sovereign and the Laws

The first and most important consequence of the principles above established is that only the general will can direct the forces of the state towards the aim of its institution, which is the common good; for if the antagonism of particular interests has rendered necessary the establishment of political societies, it is the accord of these interests that has rendered such societies possible.

I maintain, then, that sovereignty, being the exercise of the general will, cannot be alienated and that the sovereign, which is simply a collective being, cannot be represented save by itself; it may transfer its power, but not its will.

For the same reason that sovereignty is inalienable it is indivisible. For the will is either general, or it is not. If it is general, it is, when declared, an act of the people and becomes law; if it is not general, it is, when declared, merely an act of a particular person or persons, not of the sovereign.

A law is an expression of the general will and must be general in its terms and import. The sovereign cannot legislate for part of the individuals composing a state, for if it did so the general will would enter into a particular relation with particular people, and that is contrary to its nature. The law may thus confer privileges, but must not name the persons to whom the privileges are to belong; it may establish a royal government, but must not nominate a king. Any function relating to an individual object does not appertain to the legislative power.

As a popular assembly is not always enlightened in its judgements—though the general will, when properly ascertained, must be right—the service of a wise legislator is necessary to draw up laws for the sovereign's approval.

The legislator, if he be truly wise, will not begin by writing down laws that are good in the abstract, but will first look about to see whether the people for whom he intends them is capable of upholding them. He must bear in mind many considerations—the situation of the country, the nature of the soil, the density of the population, the national history, occupations and aptitudes.

Among these considerations one of the most important is the area of the state. As nature has given limits to the stature of a normal man, beyond which she makes only giants or dwarfs, there are also limits beyond which a state is, in the one direction, too large to be well governed, and, in the other too small to maintain itself. There is in every body politic a maximum of force which cannot be exceeded, and from which the state often falls away by the process of enlarging itself. The further the social bond is extended, the slacker it becomes; and, in general, a small state is proportionately stronger than a large one.

It is true that a state must have a certain breadth of base for the sake of solidity and in order to resist violent shocks from without. But, on the other hand, administration becomes more troublesome with distance. It increases in burdensomeness, moreover, with the multiplication of degrees. Each town, district and province has its administration, for which the people must pay. Finally, overwhelming everything, is the remote central administration.

Again, the government in a large state has less vigour and swiftness than in a small one; the people have less affection for their chiefs, for their country and for each other—since they are, for the most part, strangers to each other. Uniform laws are not suitable for diverse provinces; yet diverse laws among people belonging to the same state breed weakness and confusion.

The greatest good of all, which should be the aim of every system of legislation, may on investigation be reduced to two main objects—*liberty* and *equality:* liberty, because all dependence of individuals on other individuals is so much force taken away from the body of the state; equality, because without it liberty cannot exist.

III-The Government

Every free action has two causes which concur to produce it; one of them the will that determines upon the act, the other the power that performs it. In the political body one must distinguish between these two—the legislative power and the executive power. The executive power cannot belong to the sovereign, inasmuch as executive acts are particular acts, aimed at individuals, and therefore, as already explained, outside the sovereign's sphere. Public force, then, requires an agent to apply it according to the direction of the general will.

This is the government, erroneously confounded with the sovereign, of which it is only the minister. It is an intermediary body established between subjects and sovereign for their mutual correspondence, for the execution of the laws and the maintenance of civil and political liberty.

The magistrates who form the government may be numerous, or may be few; and, generally speaking, the fewer the magistrates the stronger the government. A magistrate has three wills—his personal will, his will as one of the governors and his will as a member of the sovereign. The last-named is the weakest, the first-named the most powerful.

If there is only one governor, the two stronger wills are concentrated in one man; with a few governors, they are concentrated in few men; when the government is in the hands of all the citizens, the second will be obliterated and the first widely distributed, and the government is consequently weak.

On the other hand, where there are many governors the government will be more readily kept in correspondence with the general will. The duty of the legislator is to hit the happy medium at which the government, while not failing in strength, is yet properly submissive to the sovereign.

The sovereign may, in the first place, entrust the government to the whole people or the greater part of them; this form is called democracy. Or it may be placed in the hands of a minority, in which case it is called aristocracy. Or it may be concentrated in the hands of a single magistrate from whom all the others derive their power; this is called monarchy.

It may be urged, on behalf of democracy, that those who make the laws know better than anybody how they should be interpreted and administered. But it is not right that the makers of the laws should execute them, nor that the main body of the people should turn its attention from general views to particular objects. Nothing is more dangerous than the influence of private interests on public affairs. A true democracy, in the vigorous sense of the term, never has existed and never will. It is against nature that the many should govern and the few be governed. A people composed of gods would govern itself democratically.

There are three forms of aristocracy—natural, elective and hereditary. The first is only adapted to simple peoples; the third is the worst of all governments; the second is the best of all. By the elective method, probity, sagacity and experience afford guarantees that the community will be wisely governed.

The first defect of monarchy is that it is to the interest of the monarch to keep the people in a state of weakness and misery, so that they may be unable to resist his power. Another is that under a monarchy the posts of honour are occupied by bunglers and rascals who win their promotion by petty court intrigue. Again, an elective monarchy is a cause of disorder whenever a king dies; and a hereditary monarchy leaves the character of the king to chance, which generally goes astray.

Since the sovereign has no power except its legislative authority, it only acts by laws; and since the laws are simply the authentic acts of the general will, the sovereign cannot act save when the people are assembled. It is essential that there should be definitely fixed periodic assemblies of the people that cannot be abolished or delayed, so that on the appointed day the people will be legitimately convoked by the law.

But between the sovereign authority and arbitrary government there is sometimes introduced a middle power, of which I ought to speak. As soon as the public services cease to be the main interest of the citizens, as soon as they prefer to serve their purses rather than themselves, the state is nearing its ruin. The weakening of patriotism, the activity of private interests, the immensity of states, conquests, and the abuse of government have led to the device of deputies or representatives of the people in the national assemblies. But sovereignty cannot be represented, even as it cannot be alienated; it consists essentially in the general will, and the will is not ascertainable by representation; it is either itself, or something else; there is no middle course. A law not ratified by the people in person is no law at all. The English people believes itself free, but it greatly deceives itself; it is not so, except during the election of members of parliament. As soon as they are elected, it is enslaved.

How are we to conceive the act by which the government is instituted? The first process is the determination of the sovereign that the government shall assume such and such a form; this is the establishment of a law. The second process is the nomination by the people of those to whom the government is to be entrusted; this is not a law, but a function of government.

It is a logical sequence of the social contract that in the assemblies of the people the voice of the majority prevails. The only law requiring unanimity is the contract itself. But how can a man be free, and at the same time submit to laws to which he has not consented?

I reply that when a law is proposed in the popular assembly the question put is not precisely whether the citizens approve or disapprove of it, but whether it conforms or not to the general will. The minority, then, simply have it proved to them that they estimated the general will wrongly. Once it is declared, they are, as citizens, participants in it, and as subjects they must obey it.

DAVID HUME

(1711-1776)

"A wise man proportions his belief to the evidence."

David Hume was born in Scotland in 1711, placing him squarely in the center of the Enlightenment. He was a child prodigy who graduated from Edinburgh at the age of eighteen. Hume was a good friend of Adam Smith, a fellow Scotsman. He spent time in France where he befriended the French philosopher Jean Jacques Rousseau. Unfortunately, his friendship with Rousseau would not last because of Rousseau's paranoia. Hume eventually gained recognition among European intellectuals as a writer of philosophy. He became associated with the philosophical schools of skepticism and empiricism.

Hume's philosophy brings into question what can be known with certainty. He concludes that we are essentially guided only by our sense perceptions, which can give us no certainty about the world we reside in. He goes so far as to say the experience we have of ourselves is but a sense experience, and cannot be explained on purely rational grounds. Cause and effect, according to Hume are but habits we observe and are not certainties. Hume's skeptical approach to all epistemological questions was extended to questions of ethics as well. Hume's *Essays, Moral and Political* represents an attempt to bring the skeptical view of philosophy to moral philosophy. He posits a utilitarian viewpoint as the basis for moral values, right and wrong being not a rational concept but a result of what makes one happy.

Hume's utilitarian views would influence nineteenth century thinkers such as Jeremy Bentham and John Stuart Mill. Although criticized for advocating a nihilistic view of life, Hume explained his philosophy as being positive, in so much as it was based on a principle of happiness.

ESSAYS, MORAL AND POLITICAL

DAVID HUME

I-Doubts Concerning the Understanding

All the objects of human reason or inquiry may naturally be divided into two kinds—to wit, *relations of ideas* and *matters of fact.* Of the first kind are the sciences of geometry, algebra and arithmetic, and, in short, every affirmation which is either intuitively or demonstratively certain. 'That the square of the hypotenuse is equal to the squares of the two sides' is a proposition which expresses a relation between these figures. 'That three times five is equal to the half of thirty' expresses a relation between these numbers.

Propositions of this kind are discoverable by the mere operation of thought, without dependence on what is anywhere existent in the universe. Though there never were a circle or triangle in nature, the truths demonstrated by Euclid would for ever retain their certainty and evidence.

Matters of fact, which are the second objects of human reason, are not ascertained in the same manner; nor is our evidence of their truth, however great, of a like nature with the foregoing. The contrary of every matter of fact is still possible because it can never imply a contradiction, and is conceived by the mind with the same facility and distinctness as if ever so conformable to reality. 'That the sun will not rise tomorrow' is no less intelligible a proposition, and implies no more contradiction, than the affirmative that 'it will rise.' We should in vain, therefore, attempt to demonstrate its falsehood. Were it demonstratively false, it would imply a contradiction and could never be distinctly conceived by the mind.

It may, therefore, be a subject worthy of curiosity to inquire what is the nature of that evidence which assures us of any real existence of matters of fact beyond the present testimony of our senses, or the records of our memory. All reasonings concerning matter of fact seem to be founded on the relation of *cause* and *effect*. If we would satisfy ourselves, therefore, concerning the nature of that evidence which assures us of matters of fact, we must inquire how we arrive at the knowledge of cause and effect.

I shall venture to affirm, as a general proposition which admits of no exception, that the knowledge of this relation is not, in any instance, attained by reasonings *a priori,* but arises entirely from experience.

To convince us that all the laws of nature, and all the operations of bodies without exception, are known only by experience, the following reflections may perhaps suffice. Were any object presented to us, and were we required to pronounce concerning the effect which will result from it, without consulting past observation, after what manner, I beseech you, must the mind proceed in this operation? It must invent or imagine some event, which it ascribes to the object as its effect; and it is plain that this invention must be entirely arbitrary. The mind can never possibly find the effect in the supposed cause by the most accurate examination. For the effect is totally different from the cause, and, consequently can never be discovered in it.

A stone or piece of metal raised into the air and left without any support immediately falls. But, to consider the matter *a priori,* is there anything we discover in this situation which can beget the idea of a downward rather than an upward or any other motion in the stone or metal?

In a word, then, every effect is a distinct event from its cause. It could not, therefore, be discovered in the cause, and the first invention or conception of it, *a priori,* must be entirely arbitrary. And, even after it is suggested, the conjunction of it with the cause must appear equally arbitrary, since there are always many other effects which to reason must seem fully as consistent and natural. In vain, therefore, should we pretend to infer any cause or effect, without the assistance of observation and experience.

Hence, we may discover the reason why no philosopher who is rational and modest has ever pretended to assign the ultimate cause of any natural operation, or to show distinctly the action of that power which produces any single effect in the universe.

I say, then, that even after we have experience of the operations of cause and effect, our conclusions from that experience are *not* founded on reasoning.

The bread which I formerly ate nourished me; that is, a body of such sensible qualities was at that time endued with such secret powers; but does it follow that other bread must also nourish me at another time, and that like sensible qualities must always be attended with like secret powers? The consequence seems nowise necessary. At least, it must be acknowledged that there is here a consequence drawn by the mind, that there is a certain step taken; a process of thought, and an inference which wants to be explained.

These two propositions are far from being the same: 'I have found that such an object has always been attended with such an effect,' and: 'I foresee that other objects, which are in appearance similar, will be attended with similar effects.' I shall allow, if you please, that the one proposition may justly be inferred from the other; I know, in fact, that it always is inferred. But you must confess that the inference is not intuitive; neither is it demonstrative. Of what nature is it, then? To say it is experimental is beginning the question. For all inferences from experience suppose, as their foundation, that the future will resemble the past and that similar powers will be conjoined with similar sensible qualities.

If there be any suspicion that the course of nature may change and that the past may be no rule for the future, all experience becomes useless and can give rise to no inference or conclusion. It is impossible, therefore, that any arguments from experience can prove this resemblance of the past to the future, since all these arguments are founded on the supposition of that resemblance. Let the course of things be allowed hitherto ever so regular, that alone, without some new argument or inference, proves not that for the future it will continue so.

In vain do you pretend to have learnt the nature of bodies from your past experience. Their secret nature, and consequently all their effects and influence, may change without any change in their sensible qualities. This happens sometimes, and with regard to some objects. Why may it not happen always, and with regard to all objects? What logic, what process of argument, secures you against this supposition?

My practice, you say, refutes my doubts. But you mistake the purport of my question. As an agent, I am quite satisfied on the point; but as a philosopher, who has some share of curiosity, I will not say scepticism, I want to learn the foundation of this inference.

All inferences from experience are effects of custom, not of reasoning. We have already observed that nature has established connexions among particular ideas, and that no sooner one idea occurs to our thoughts than it introduces its correlative, and carries our attention towards it by a gentle and insensible movement. These principles of connexion or association we have reduced to three—namely, *resemblance, contiguity* and *causation,* which are the only bonds that unite our thoughts together and beget that regular train of reflection or discourse which, in a greater or less degree, takes place among mankind.

Now, here arises a question on which the solution of the present difficulty will depend. Does it happen in all these relations that when one of the objects is presented to the senses or memory the mind is not only carried to the conception of the correlative, but reaches a steadier and stronger conception of it than otherwise it would have been able to attain? This seems to be the case with that belief which arises from the relation of cause and effect.

And I shall add that it is conformable to the ordinary wisdom of nature to secure so necessary an act of the mind by some instinct or mechanical tendency, which may be infallible in its operations, may discover itself at the first appearance of thought, and may be independent of the laboured deductions of the understanding.

II-On Miracles

A wise man proportions his belief to the evidence. In such conclusions as are founded on an infallible experience he expects the event with the last degree of assurance as a full *proof* of the future existence of that event.

In other cases he proceeds with more caution. He weighs the opposite experiments. He considers which side is supported by the greatest number of experiments; to that side he inclines with doubt and hesitation, and when at last he fixes his judgment, the evidence exceeds not what we properly call *probability.* All probability, then, supposes an opposition of experiments and observations, where the one side is found to over-balance the other and to produce a degree of evidence proportioned to the superiority.

When the fact attested is such a one as has seldom fallen under our observation, there is a contest of two possible experiences, of which the one destroys the other as far as its force goes, and the superior can only operate on the mind by the force which remains. The very same principle of experience which gives us a certain degree of assurance in the testimony of witnesses gives us also, in this case, another degree of assurance against the fact which they endeavour to establish, from which consideration there necessarily arises a counterpoise, and mutual destruction of belief and authority.

But in order to increase the probability against the testimony of witnesses, let us suppose that the fact which they affirm, instead of being only marvellous, is really miraculous; and suppose also that the testimony, considered apart and in itself, amounts to an entire proof, of which the strongest must prevail, but still with a diminution of its force in proportion to that of its antagonist.

A miracle is a violation of the laws of nature; and as a firm and unalterable experience has established these laws, the proof against a miracle, from the very nature of the fact, is as entire as any argument from experience can possibly be imagined. Why is it more than probable that all men must die; that lead cannot of itself remain suspended in the air; that fire consumes wood, and is extinguished by water; unless it be that these events are found agreeable to the laws of nature, and there is required a violation of these laws, or, in other words, a miracle, to prevent them?

Nothing is esteemed a miracle if it ever happen in the common course of nature. It is no miracle that a man seemingly in good health should die on a sudden, because such a kind of death, though more unusual than any other, has yet been frequently observed to happen. But it is a miracle that a dead man should come to life, because that has never been observed in any age or country.

There must, therefore, be a uniform experience against every miraculous event, otherwise the event would not merit that appellation. And as a uniform experience amounts to a proof, there is here a direct and full *proof,* from the nature of the fact, against the existence of any miracle; nor can such a proof be destroyed, or the miracle rendered credible, but by an opposite proof which is superior.

The plain consequence is (and it is a general maxim worthy of our attention) 'that no testimony is sufficient to establish a miracle unless the testimony be of such a kind that its falsehood would be more miraculous than the fact which it endeavours to establish; and even in that case there is a mutual destruction of arguments, and the superior only gives us an assurance suitable to that degree of force which remains after deducting the inferior.'

There surely never was a greater number of miracles ascribed to one person than those which were lately said to have been wrought in France upon the tomb of Abbé Paris, the famous Jansenist, with whose sanctity the people were so long deluded. The curing of the sick, giving hearing to the deaf and sight to the blind, were everywhere talked of as the usual effects of that holy sepulchre. But, what is more extraordinary, many of the miracles were immediately proved upon the spot before judges of unquestioned integrity, attested by witnesses of credit and distinction, in a learned age, and in the most eminent theatre that is now in the world.

Nor is this all; a relation of them was published and dispersed everywhere; nor were the Jesuits, though a learned body, supported by the civil magistrate and determined enemies to those opinions in whose favour the miracles were said to have been wrought, ever able distinctly to refute or detect them. Where shall we find such a number of circumstances agreeing to the corroboration of one fact? And what have we to oppose to such a cloud of witnesses but the absolute impossibility or miraculous nature of the events which they relate? And this surely, in the eyes of all reasonable people, will alone be regarded as a sufficient refutation.

Suppose that all the historians who treat of England should agree that on January 1, 1600, Queen Elizabeth died; that both before and after her death she was seen by her physicians and the whole court, as is usual with persons of her rank; that her successor was acknowledged and proclaimed by the Parliament; and that, after being interred a month, she again appeared, resumed the throne and governed England for three years; I must confess that I should be surprised at the concurrence of so many odd circumstances, but should not have the least inclination to believe so miraculous an event. I should not doubt of her pretended death, and of those other public circumstances that followed it; I should only assert it to have been pretended, and that it neither was, nor possibly could be, real.

You would in vain object to me the difficulty and almost impossibility of deceiving the world in an affair of such consequence; the wisdom and solid judgement of that renowned queen; with the little or no advantage which she could reap from so poor an artifice. All this might astonish me; but I would still reply that the knavery and folly of men are such common phenomena that I should rather believe the most extraordinary events to arise from their concurrence than admit of so signal a violation of the laws of nature.

Our most holy religion is founded on *faith*, not on reason; and it is a sure method of exposing it to put it to such a trial as it is by no means fitted to endure. To make this more evident, let us examine those miracles related in the Pentateuch, which we shall examine as the production of a mere human writer and historian. Here, then, we are first to consider a book, presented to us by a barbarous and ignorant people, written in an age when they were still more barbarous, and in all probability long after the facts which it relates, corroborated by no concurring testimony, and resembling those fabulous accounts which every nation gives of its origin.

Upon reading this book, we find it full of prodigies and miracles. It gives an account of a state of the world and of human nature entirely different from the present; of our fall from that state; of the age of man extended to near a thousand years; of the destruction of the world by a deluge; of the arbitrary choice of one people as the favourites of Heaven, and that people the countrymen of the author; of their deliverance from bondage by prodigies the most astonishing imaginable. I desire anyone to lay his hand upon his heart and, after a serious consideration, declare whether he thinks that the falsehood of such a book, supported by such a testimony, would be more extraordinary and miraculous than the miracles it relates, which is, however, necessary to make it be received according to the measures of probability above established.

III-Of A Particular Providence and of A Future State

I was lately engaged in conversation with a friend who loves sceptical paradoxes. To my expression of the opinion that a wise magistrate can justly be jealous of certain tenets of philosophy such as those of Epicurus, which, denying a divine existence, and consequently a Providence and a future state, seem to loosen the ties of morality, he replied:

"If Epicurus had been accused before the people he could easily have defended his cause and proved his principles of philosophy to be as salutary as those of his adversaries. And, if you please, I shall suppose myself Epicurus for a moment, and make you stand for the Athenian people."

"Very well; pray proceed upon these suppositions."

Epicurus: I come hither, O ye Athenians, to justify in your assembly what I maintained in my school, and I find myself impeached by furious antagonists instead of reasoning with calm and dispassionate inquirers.

By my accusers it is acknowledged that the chief or sole argument for a divine existence (which I never questioned) is derived from the order of nature; where there appear such marks of intelligence and design that you think it extravagant to assign for its cause either chance or the blind and unguided force of matter. You allow that this is an argument drawn from effects to causes. From the order of the work you infer that there must have been project and forethought in the workman. If you cannot make out this point, you allow that your conclusion fails, and you pretend not to establish the conclusion in a greater latitude than the phenomena of nature will justify. These are your concessions. Please mark the consequences.

When we infer any particular cause from an effect we must proportion the one to the other, and can never be allowed to ascribe to the cause any qualities but what are sufficient to produce the effect. A body of ten ounces raised in a scale may serve as a proof that the counter-balancing weight exceeds ten ounces, but never that it exceeds a hundred.

The same rule holds whether the cause assigned by brute, unconscious matter or a rational, intelligent being. If the cause be known only by the effect, we never ought to ascribe to it any qualities beyond what are precisely requisite to produce the effect. Nor can we return from the cause and infer other effects from it beyond those by which alone it is known to us.

Allowing, therefore, the gods to be the authors of the existence, or order, of the universe, it follows that they possess that precise degree of power, intelligence and benevolence which appears in their workmanship; but nothing farther can ever be proved except we call in the assistance of exaggeration and flattery to supply the defects of argument and reasoning. So far as the traces of any attributes at present appear, so far may we conclude these attributes to exist. The supposition of further attributes is mere hypothesis; much more the supposition that in distant regions of space, or periods of time, there has been, or will be, a more magnificent display of these attributes and a scheme of administration more suitable to such imaginary virtues.

We can never be allowed to mount up from the universe, the effect, to Jupiter, the cause, and then descend downwards to infer any new effect from that cause. The knowledge of the cause being derived solely from the effect, they must be exactly adjusted to each other; and the one can never refer to anything farther.

I deny a Providence, you say, and Supreme Governor of the world, who guides the course of events and punishes the vicious with infamy and disappointment, and rewards the virtuous with honour and success in all their undertakings. But surely I deny not the course of events itself, which lies open to everyone's inquiry and examination. I acknowledge that, in the present order of things, virtue is attended with more peace of mind than vice, and meets with a more favourable reception from the world. I am sensible that, according to the past experience of mankind, friendship is the chief joy of human life, and moderation the only source of tranquility and happiness. I never balance between the virtuous and the vicious life, but am sensible that, to a well-disposed mind, every advantage is on the side of the former. And what can you say more, for all your suppositions and reasonings?

IMMANUEL KANT

(1724-1804)

"So act as to treat humanity, whether in thine own person or in that of any other, in every case as an end withal, never as means only."

H.J. Paton, American scholar, said about "Fundamental Principles of the Metaphysics of Morals" that it is an indispensable book for all who profess to think seriously about moral problems." Such an observation almost a century and a half after the death of Immanuel Kant, testifies to the significant place the German philosopher holds in the history of metaphysics and ethics. Because Kant's work is difficult to read, his abstract concepts have been subject to distortion and misrepresentation by both his admirers and detractors.

Three longer works, *Critique of Pure Reason*, *Critique of Practical Reason*, and *Critique of Judgement*, established Kant's enduring place in philosophy as he attempted to offer explanations about faith, freedom, and immortality. His failure to provide satisfactory conclusions to the questions he raised fades in the face of the contribution he made in forcing the discussion of these human concerns to levels that did not exist before him.

The passage included here points to the challenges that the philosopher's style presents to the reader, but it also contains one of the most famous of his concepts—the categorical imperative.

FUNDAMENTAL PRINCIPLES OF THE METAPHYSIC OF MORALS

IMMANUEL KANT

When I conceive a hypothetical imperative, in general I do not know beforehand what it will contain until I am given the condition. But when I conceive a categorical imperative, I know at once what it contains. For as the imperative contains besides the law only the necessity that the maxims shall conform to this law, while the law contains no conditions restricting it, there remains nothing but the general statement that the maxim of the action should conform to a universal law, and it is this conformity alone that the imperative properly represents as necessary.

There is therefore but one categorical imperative, namely, this: *Act only on that maxim whereby thou canst at the same time will that it should become a universal law.*

Now if all imperatives of duty can be deduced from this one imperative as from their principle, then, although it should remain undecided whether what is called duty is not merely a vain notion, yet at least we shall be able to show what we understand by it and what this notion means.

Since the universality of the law according to which effects are produced constitutes what is properly called *nature* in the most general sense (as to form)—that is, the existence of things so far as it is determined by general laws—the imperative of duty may be expressed thus:

Act as if the maxim of thy action were to become by thy will a universal law of nature.

We will now enumerate a few duties, adopting the usual division of them into duties to ourselves and to others, and into perfect and imperfect duties.

1. A man reduced to despair by a series of misfortunes feels wearied of life, but is still so far in possession of his reason that he can ask himself whether it would not be contrary to his duty to himself to take his own life. Now he inquires whether the maxim of his action could become a universal law of nature. His maxim is: From self-love I adopt it as a principle to shorten my life when its longer duration is likely to bring more evil than satisfaction. It is asked then simply whether this principle founded on self-love can become a universal law of nature. Now we see at once that a system of nature of which it should be a law to destroy life by means of the very feeling whose special nature it is to impel to the improvement of life would contradict itself, and therefore could not exist as a system of nature; hence that maxim cannot possibly exist as a universal law of nature, and consequently would be wholly inconsistent with the supreme principle of all duty.

2. Another finds himself forced by necessity to borrow money. He knows that he will not be able to repay it, but sees also that nothing will be lent to him unless he promises stoutly to repay it in a definite time. He desires to make this promise, but he has still so much conscience as to ask himself: Is it not unlawful and inconsistent with duty to get out of a difficulty in this way? Suppose, however, that he resolves to do so, then the maxim of his action would be expressed thus: When I think myself in want of money, I will borrow money and promise to repay it, although I know that I never can do so. Now this principle of self-love or of one's own advantage may perhaps be consistent with my whole future welfare; but the question now is, Is it right? I change then the suggestion of self-love into a universal law, and state the question thus: How would it be if my maxim were a universal law? Then I see at once that it could never hold as a universal law of nature, but would necessarily contradict itself. For supposing it to be a universal law that everyone when he thinks himself in a difficulty should be able to promise whatever he pleases with the purpose of not keeping his promise, the promise itself would become impossible, as well as the end that one might have in view of it, since no one would consider that anything was promised to him, but would ridicule all such statements as vain pretenses.

3. A third finds himself a talent which with the help of some culture might make him a useful man in many respects. But he finds himself in comfortable circumstances and prefers to indulge in pleasure rather than to take pains in enlarging and improving his happy natural capacities. He asks, however, whether his maxim of neglect of his natural gifts, besides agreeing with his inclination to indulgence, agrees also with what is called duty. He sees then that a system of nature could indeed subsist with such a universal law, although men (like the South Sea islanders) should let their talents rest and resolve to devote their lives merely to idleness, amusement, and propagation of their species—in a word, to enjoyment; but he cannot possibly *will* that this should be a universal law of nature, or be implanted in us as such by a natural instinct. For, as a rational being, he necessarily wills that his faculties be developed, since they serve him, and have been given him, for all sorts of possible purposes.

4. A fourth, who is in prosperity, while he sees that others have to contend with great wretchedness and that he could help them, thinks: What concern is it of mine? Let everyone be as happy as Heaven pleases, or as he can make himself; I will take nothing from him nor even envy him, only I do not wish to contribute anything to his welfare or to his assistance in distress! Now no doubt, if such a mode of thinking were a universal law, the human race might very well subsist, and doubtless even better than in a state in which everyone talks of sympathy and good-will, or even takes care occasionally to put it into practice, but, on the other side, also cheats when he can, betrays the rights of men, or otherwise violates them. But although it is possible that a universal law of nature might exist in accordance with that maxim, it is impossible to *will* that such a principle should have the universal validity of a law of nature. For a will which resolved this would contradict itself, inasmuch as many cases might occur in which one would have need of the love and sympathy of others, and in which, by such a law of nature, sprung from his own will, he would deprive himself of all hope of the aid he desires.

These are a few of the many actual duties, or at least what we regard as such, which obviously fall into two classes on the one principle that we have laid down. We must be *able to will* that a maxim of our action should be a universal law. This is the canon of the moral appreciation of the action generally. Some actions are of such a character that their maxim cannot without contradiction be even *conceived* as a universal law of nature, far from it being possible that we should *will* that it *should* be so. In others, this intrinsic impossibility is not found, but still it is impossible to *will* that their maxim should be raised to the universality of a law of nature, since such a will would contradict itself. It is easily seen that the former violate strict or rigorous (inflexible) duty; the latter only laxer (meritorious) duty. Thus it has been completely shown by these examples how all duties depend as regards the nature of the obligation (not the object of the action) on the same principle.

The question then is this: Is it a necessary law *for all rational beings* that they should always judge of their actions by maxims of which they can themselves will that they should serve as universal laws? If it is so, then it must be connected (altogether *a priori*) with the very conception of the will of a rational being generally. But in order to discover this connection we must, however reluctantly, take a step into metaphysic, although into a domain of it which is distinct from speculative philosophy—namely, the metaphysic of morals. In a practical philosophy, where it is not the reasons of what *happens* that we have to ascertain, but the laws of what *ought to happen,* even although it never does, that is, objective practical laws, there it is not necessary to inquire into the reasons why anything pleases or displeases, how the pleasure of mere sensation differs from taste, and whether the latter is distinct from a general satisfaction of reason; on what the feeling of pleasure or pain rests, and how from it desires and inclinations arise, and from these again maxims by the cooperation of reason; for all this belongs to an empirical psychology, which would constitute the second part of physics, if we regard physics as the *philosophy* of nature, so far as it is based on *empirical laws.* But here we are concerned with objective practical laws, and consequently with the relation of the will to itself so far as it is determined by reason alone, in which case whatever has reference to anything empirical is necessarily excluded; since if *reason of itself alone* determines the conduct (and it is the possibility of this that we are now investigating), it must necessarily do so *a priori.*

The will is conceived as a faculty of determining oneself to action *in accordance with the conception of certain laws.* And such a faculty can be found only in rational beings. Now that which serves the will as the objective ground of its self-determination is the *end,* and if this is assigned by reason alone, it must hold for all rational beings. On the other hand, that which merely contains the ground of possibility of the action of which the effect is the end, this is called the *means*. The subjective ground of the desire is the *spring*, the objective ground of the volition is the *motive;* hence the distinction between subjective ends which rest on springs, and objective ends which depend on motives valid for every rational being. Practical principles are *formal* when they abstract from all subjective ends; they are *material* when they assume these, and therefore particular, springs of action. The ends which a rational being proposes to himself at pleasure as *effects* of his actions (material ends) are all only relative, for it is only their relation to the particular desires of the subject that gives them their worth, which therefore cannot furnish principles universal and necessary for all rational beings and for every volition, that is to say, practical laws. Hence all these relative ends can give rise only to hypothetical imperatives.

Supposing, however, that there were something *whose existence* has *in itself* an absolute worth, something which, being *an end in itself,* could be a source of definite laws, then in this and this alone would lie the source of a possible categorical imperative, that is, a practical law.

Now I say: man and generally any rational being *exists* as an end in himself, *not merely as a means* to be arbitrarily used by this or that will, but in all his actions, whether they concern himself or other rational beings, must be always regarded at the same time as an end. All objects of the inclinations have only a conditional worth; for if the inclinations and the wants founded on them did not exist, then their object would be without value. But the inclinations themselves, being sources of want, are so far from having an absolute worth for which they should be desired that, on the contrary, it must be the universal wish of every rational being to be wholly free from them. Thus the worth of any object which is *to be acquired* by our action is always conditional. Beings whose existence depends not on our will but on nature's, have nevertheless, if they are nonrational beings, only a relative value as means, and are therefore called *things;* rational beings, on the contrary, are called *persons,* because their very nature points them out as ends in themselves, that is, as something which must not be used merely as means, and so far therefore restricts freedom of action (and is an object of respect). These, therefore, are not merely subjective ends whose existence has a worth *for us* as an effect of our action, but *objective ends,* that is, things whose existence is an end in itself—an end, moreover, for which no other can be substituted, which they should subserve *merely* as means, for otherwise nothing whatever would possess *absolute worth;* but if all worth were conditioned and therefore contingent, then there would be no supreme practical principle of reason whatever.

If then there is a supreme practical principle or, in respect of the human will, a categorical imperative, it must be one which, being drawn from the conception of that which is necessarily an end for everyone because it is *an end in itself,* constitutes an *objective* principle of will, and can therefore serve as a universal practical law. The foundation of this principle is: *rational nature exists as an end in itself.* Man necessarily conceives his own existence as being so; so far then this is a *subjective* principle of human actions. But every other rational being regards its existence similarly, just on the same rational principle that holds for me; so that it is at the same time an objective principle from which as a supreme practical law all laws of the will must be capable of being deduced. Accordingly the practical imperative will be as follows: *So act as to treat humanity, whether in thine own person or in that of any other, in every case as an end withal, never as means only.* We will now inquire whether this can be practically carried out.

To abide by the previous examples:

First, under the head of necessary duty to oneself: He who contemplates suicide should ask himself whether his action can be consistent with the idea of humanity *as an end in itself.* If he destroys himself in order to escape from painful circumstances, he uses a person merely as *a mean* to maintain a tolerable condition up to the end of life. But a man is not a thing, that is to say, something which can be used merely as means, but must in all his actions be always considered as an end in himself. I cannot, therefore, dispose in any way of a man in my own person so as to mutilate him, to damage or kill him. (It belongs to ethics proper to define this principle more precisely, so as to avoid all misunderstanding, for example, as to the amputation of the limbs in order to preserve myself; as to exposing my life to danger with a view to preserve it, etc. This question is therefore omitted here.)

Secondly, as regards necessary duties, or those of strict obligation, towards others: He who is thinking of making a lying promise to others will see at once that he would be using another man *merely as a mean,* without the latter containing at the same time the end in himself. For he whom I propose by such a promise to use for my own purposes cannot possible assent to my mode of acting towards him, and therefore cannot himself contain the end of this action. This violation of the principles of humanity in other men is more obvious if we take in examples of attacks on the freedom and property of others. For then it is clear that he who transgresses the rights of men intends to use the person of others merely as means, without considering that as rational beings they ought always to be esteemed also as ends, that is, as beings who must be capable of containing in themselves the end of the very same action.

Thirdly, as regards contingent (meritorious) duties to oneself: It is not enough that the action does not violate humanity in our own person as an end in itself, it must also *harmonize with* it. Now there are in humanity capacities of greater perfection which belong to the end that nature has in view in regard to humanity in ourselves as the subject; to neglect these might perhaps be consistent with the *maintenance* of humanity as an end in itself, but not with the *advancement* of this end.

Fourthly, as regards meritorious duties towards others: The natural end which all men have is their own happiness. Now humanity might indeed subsist although no one should contribute anything to the happiness of others, provided he did not intentionally withdraw anything from it; but after all, this would only harmonize negatively, not positively, with *humanity as an end in itself,* if everyone does not also endeavor, as far as in him lies, to forward the ends of others. For the ends of any subject which is an end in himself ought as far as possible to be *my* ends also, if that conception is to have its *full* effect with me.

GEORG WILHELM FRIEDRICH HEGEL

(1770-1831)

"Philosophy is, in consequence, identical with religion"

Hegel was born in 1770 in Stuttgart, Germany. The course of Hegel's life encompassed the French Revolution, the Napoleonic Era, and the rise of the state of Prussia. Hegel was deeply influenced by these events and developed a comprehensive theory of history to help explain the movements of history. He became a university professor at Jena, where he developed his great philosophical work, *The Phenomenology of Mind*. In this work, Hegel posited that "the real is the rational, and the rational is the real." All of history, according to Hegel, can be explained by consciousness (spirit/the absolute) trying to realize itself. The movement of history is the movement of the spirit towards full realization. The individual counts for very little in Hegel's system. Only truly great men (such as Napoleon) play any significant role in history.

In Hegel's *The Philosophy of Religion,* he equates spirit with God. The role of history, or so it seems, is for God to come to a full realization of himself. Hegel has been criticized for having a particularly difficult style of writing. *The Philosophy of Religion* serves as a good example of Hegel's writing style.

THE PHILOSOPHY OF RELIGION

G.W.F. HEGEL

I-The Relation of Philosophy to Religion

The object of religion is the same as that of philosophy; it is the eternal verity itself in its objective existence; it is God. Nothing but God and the unfolding of God. Philosophy is not the wisdom of the world, but the knowledge of things which are not of this world. It is not the knowledge of external mass, of empirical life and existence, but of the eternal, of the nature of God, and of all which flows from His nature. For this nature ought to manifest and develop itself. Consequently, philosophy in unfolding religion merely unfolds itself, and in unfolding itself it unfolds religion.

In so far as philosophy is occupied with the eternal truth, the truth which is in and for itself; in so far as it is occupied with this as thinking spirit, rather than in an arbitrary fashion and in view of a particular interest, philosophy has the same sphere of activity as has religion. And if the religious consciousness aspires to abolish all that is peculiar to itself and to be absorbed in its object, the philosophic spirit likewise plunges with the same energy into its object and renounces all particularity.

Religion and philosophy are thus at one in having one and the same object. Philosophy, in fact, also is the adoration of God, it is religion; for, seeing that God is its object, it involves the same renunciation of every opinion and every thought that is arbitrary and subjective. Philosophy is, in consequence, identical with religion. Only it is religion in a peculiar manner, and this it is which distinguishes it from religion commonly so called. So philosophy and religion are both religion, and that which distinguishes one from the other is no more than the characteristic mode in which respectively they consider their object, God.

Here is the difficulty of understanding how philosophy can make but one with religion, a difficulty which has even been mistaken for impossibility. Thence also arise the fears which philosophy inspires in theology and the hostile attitudes which they assume towards each other. What brings about this attitude is, on the side of theology, that for her philosophy does nothing but corrupt, pull down and profane the content of religion, and that she understands God in a totally different manner from that after which religion understands him.

It is the same opposition which long ago among the Greeks caused a free and democratic people like the Athenians to burn books and to condemn Socrates. In our own day, however, this opposition is considered a thing which it is natural to admit—more natural indeed than the other opinion concerning the unity of religion and philosophy.

Diverse religions offer us, it is true, only too often the most bizarre and monstrous representations of the divine essence. But we must not confine ourselves to a superficial consideration and consequent rejection of these representations and the religious practices which follow upon them as being engendered by superstition, by error, or by imposture, or even by a simple piety, and so neglect their essential value. There is need to discover in these representations and in these practices their relation with truth.

II-God the Universal

For us, who have a religion, God is a familiar being, a substantial truth existing in our subjective consciousness. But, scientifically considered, God is a general and abstract term. The philosophy of religion it is which develops and grasps the divine nature and which teaches us what God is. God is a familiar idea, but an idea which has still to be scientifically developed.

The result of philosophic examination is that God is the absolute truth, the universal in and for itself, embracing all things and in which all things subsist. And in regard to this assertion, we may appeal in the first place to the religious consciousness, and to its conviction that God is the absolute truth whence all things proceed, whither they all return, upon which all things depend and in respect of which nothing can possess a true and absolute independence.

The heart may very well be full of this representation of God, but science is not built up of what is in the heart. The object of science is that which has arisen to the level of consciousness, and of thinking consciousness; in other words, which has attained the form of thought.

In so much as He is the universal, God is, for us, in relation to development, Being enclosed in itself, Being at unity with itself. When we say God is Being enclosed in itself, we enunciate a proposition which is bound to a development which we await. But this envelopment of God in Himself which we have called His universality we must not conceive, relatively to God Himself and His content, as an abstract universality, outside of which, and as opposed to which, the particular has an independent existence.

So we must consider this universal as an absolute concrete universal. This sense of fullness is the sense in which God is one, and there is but one God—that is to say, God is not one merely by contrast with other gods, but because it is He that is the One, that is, God.

The things which are, the developments of the worlds of nature and of mind, show a multiplicity of forms and an infinite variety of existences. But whatever may be their difference of degree, of force, of content, these things have no true independence; their being is consequent and, so to speak, contingent. When we predicate being of particular things, it is not of absolute Being that we speak—Being of and from itself; that is, God—but a borrowed being, a semblance of being.

God is His universality—that is, this universal Being which has no limit, no bounds, no particularity—is a Being which subsists absolutely, and which subsists alone; all else which subsists has its root in this unity, and by this alone subsists. In thus representing to ourselves this first content we may say that God is absolute substance, the only veritable reality. For not everything which has a reality has a reality of its own, or subsists by itself. God is the only absolute reality, and thereby the absolute substance.

If we stop at this abstract thought we have Spinozism, for in Spinozism subjectivity is not yet differentiated from substantiality, from substance as such. But in the pre-supposition just made there is also this thought—God is spirit, absolute and eternal; spirit which comes not forth from itself in differentiation. This ideality, this subjectivity of spirit, which is transparency, ideality excluding all particular determination, is precisely the universal, pure relation to itself, Being which remains absolutely within itself.

If we halt at substance, we fail to grasp this Universal under its concrete form. In its concrete determination spirit always preserves its unity, this unity of its reality which we call substance. But one should add that this substantiality, the unity of the absolute reality with itself, is but the foundation, but a moment in the determination of God as spirit. Hence, principally, arises the reproach which is directed against philosophy—to wit, that philosophy, to be consistent with itself, is necessarily Spinozism, and consequently atheism and fatalism. But at the beginning we have not yet determinations distinguished one from another as aye and nay. We have the one but not the other.

Consequently, what we have here is, to start with, content under the form of substance. Even when we say, 'God,' 'spirit,' we have only words, indeterminate representations. The essential point is to know what has been produced in the consciousness. And that is, first, the simple, the abstract. Here, in this first simple determination, we have God only under the form of universality. Only we do not halt at this moment.

Nevertheless, this content remains the foundation of all further developments, for in these developments God comes not forth from His unity. When God creates the world—to use the expression of everyday—there comes not into existence an evil, a contrary, existing in itself independently of God.

III-God Exists for Thought

This Beginning is an object for us or a content in us. We possess this object. Immediately the question arises, Who are we? We, I, spirit—here also is a complex being, a multiplied being. I have perceptions; I see, I hear, etc. Seeing, hearing; all this is I. Consequently, the precise sense of this question is, Which among these determinations is it in accordance with which this content exists for our minds? Idea, will, imagination, feeling—which is the seat, the proper domain of this content, of this object?

If we accept the common answers to this question, God will abide in us as the object of faith, of feeling, of representation, of knowledge.

We shall have to examine more closely later on in a special fashion with respect to this point, these forms, faculties, aspects of ourselves.

In this place we shall not seek a reply to this question; nor shall we say, basing our answer on experience and observation, that God is in our feeling, etc. But, to begin with, we will confine ourselves to what we have actually before us, to this One, concrete Being.

If we take this One, and ask for what power, for what activity of our mind does this One, this absolutely universal Being, exist, we cannot but name the one activity of mind which corresponds to it as constituting its proper natural domain. This activity, which corresponds to the universal, is thought.

Thought is the field in which this content moves; it is the energising of the universal, or the universal in reality of its activity. Or, if we say that thought embraces the universal, that for which the universal is will still be thought.

This universal which can be produced by thought, and which is for thought, may be a quite abstract universal. In this sense it is the unlimited, the infinite, the being without bounds, without particular determination. This universal, negative to begin with, has its seat not elsewhere than in thought.

To think of God is to rise above the things of sense, exterior and individual, above simple feeling into the region of pure being; being at unity with itself—that is to say, into the pure region of the universal. And this region is thought.

Such is the substratum for this content considered on the subjective side. Here the content is that Being in which is no difference, no schism; Being which abides in itself, the universal; and thought is the form for which this universal is.

Thus we have a difference between thought and the universal which we have called God. It is a difference which in the first place belongs only to our reflection, and is by no means to be found in the content on its own account. There is the result to which philosophy comes—a result already comprised in religion as under the form of faith—to wit, that God is the sole veritable reality, the Being without which no other reality would exist.

In the unity of this reality, in this cloudless shining, the reality and the distinction which we call thinking-being have as yet no place.

What we have before us is this absolute unity. This content we cannot yet call religion, because to religion belongs subjective spirit, consciousness. Thought is the seat of this universal, but this seat is absorbed in this being which is one, eternal, in and for itself.

This universal constitutes the beginning and the point of departure, but only as unity which so abides. It is not a mere substratum whence differences are born; rather, all differences are included in this universal. No more is it an abstract and inert universal, but the absolute principle of all activity, the matrix, the infinite source whence all things proceed, whither all things return, and in which they are eternally preserved.

Thus the universal is never separated from this ethereal element, from this unity with itself, this concentration within itself.

IV-What is Evil?

As the universal, God could not find Himself faced by a contrary whereof the reality should pretend to rise above the phantasmal level. For this pure unity and this perfect transparency matter is nothing impenetrable, and spirit, the ego, is not so independent as to possess a true, individual substantiality.

There has been a tendency to label this idea pantheism. It would be more exact to call it the conception of substantiality. God is first determined as substance only. The absolute subject, spirit, is also substance; but it is determined rather as subject. This is the difference generally ignored by those who assert that speculative philosophy is pantheism. As usual, they miss the essential point and disparage philosophy by falsifying it.

Pantheism is commonly taken to mean that God is all things—the whole, the universe, the collection of all existences, of things finite and infinitely diverse. From which notion the charge is brought against philosophy that it teaches that all things are God; that is to say, that God is, not the universal which is in and for itself, but the infinite multiplicity of individual things in their empirical and immediate existence.

If you say God is all that is here, this paper, etc., you have indeed committed yourself to the pantheism with which philosophy is reproached; that is, the whole is understood as equivalent to all individual things. But there is also the genus, which is equally the universal, yet is wholly different from this totality in which the universal is but the collection of individual things, and the basis, the content, is constituted by these things themselves. To say that there has ever been a religion which has taught this pantheism is to say what is absolutely untrue. It has never entered any man's mind that everything is God; that is to say, that God is things in their individual and contingent existence. Far less has philosophy ever taught this doctrine.

Spinozism itself, as such, as well as Oriental pantheism, contains this doctrine: that the divine in all things is no more than that which is universal in their content, their essence; and in such sense that this essence is conceived of as a determinate essence.

When Brahma says, 'In the metal I am the brightness of its shining; among the rivers I am the Ganges; I am the life of all that lives,' he thereby suppresses the individual. He says not, 'I am the metal, the rivers, the individual things of various kinds as such, nor in the fashion of their immediate existence.'

Here, at this stage, what is expressed is no longer pantheism; but rather that of the essence in individual things.

In the living being are time and space. But in the individual being it is only the changeless element that is made to stand out. 'The life of being that lives' is in this latter sphere of life the unlimited, the universal. But if it be said 'God is all things,' here we understand individuality with all its limitations, its finity, its passing existence. This notion of pantheism arises out of the conception of unity, not as spiritual unity, but abstract unity; and then, when the idea takes its religious form, where only the substance, the One, is possessed of true reality, there is a tendency to forget that it is precisely in presence of this unity that individual and finite things are effaced, and to continue to place these in a material fashion side by side with this unity. They will not admit the teaching of the Eleatics, who, when they say 'There is only One,' add expressly that non-entity is not. All that is finite would be limitation, a negation of the One, but non-entity, the boundary, term, limit, and that which is limited, exist not at all.

Spinozism has been accused of atheism. But Spinozism does not teach that God is the world, that He is *all things.* Things have indeed a phenomenal existence—that is, an existence as appearances. We speak of our existence, and our life is indeed comprised in this existence, but to speak philosophically the world has no reality, it has no existence. Individual things are finite things to which no reality can be attributed; it may be said of them that they have no existence.

Spinozism—this is the accusation directed against it—involves by way of consequence that, if all things make but one, good and evil make but one; there is no difference between them; and thereby all religion is destroyed. In themselves, it is said there is no difference between good and evil; consequently it is a matter of indifference whether one be righteous or wicked.

It may be granted that in themselves—that is, in God, who is the sole veritable reality—the difference between good and evil disappears. In God is no evil. But the difference between good and evil can exist only on condition that God is the evil. But it cannot be allowed that evil is an affirmative thing, and that this affirmation is in God. God is good, and nothing else than good; the distinction between good and evil is not present in this unity, in this substance, and comes into existence only with differentiation.

God is unity abiding absolutely in itself. In the substance there is no differentiation. The distinction of good and evil begins with the distinction of God from the world, and particularly from man. It is the fundamental principle of Spinozism with regard to this distinction of God and the world that man must have no other end than God. The love of God, therefore, it is that Spinozism marks out for man as the law to be followed in order to bring about the healing of this breach.

And it is the loftiest morality that teaches that evil has no existence and that man is not bound to permit the substantial existence of this distinction, this negation. Yet it is possible for him to desire to maintain the difference and even to push it to the point of sheer opposition to God. In this case man is evil. But he may annul this distinction and place his true existence in God alone and in his aspiration towards Him; in this case he is good.

In Spinozism there is indeed the difference between good and evil, opposition between God and man; but side by side with it we have also the principle that evil is to be deemed a non-entity. In God as God, in God as substance, there is no distinction. It is for man that the distinction exists, as also for him exists the distinction of good and evil.

V-The Determination of Unity

The superficial method of appraising philosophy is exemplified also in those who assert that it is a 'system of identity.' It is perfectly true that substance is this unity at one with itself, but spirit no less is this self-identity. Ultimately, all is identity, unity with itself. But when they speak of the philosophy of identity they have in view abstract identity or unity in general; and they neglect the essential point, to wit, the determination of this unity in itself; in other words, they omit to consider whether this unity is determined as substance or as spirit. Philosophy from beginning to end is nothing else than the study of determinations of unity.

In the sphere of the Notion many unities are comprised. The combination of water and earth is a unity, but this unity is mixture. If we bring together a base and an acid, we have as the result a crystal; also water; but water which cannot be discerned and which gives no trace of humidity. Here the unity of the water and of this matter is a unity different from the mixture of water and earth. The essential point is the difference of these determinations. The unity of God is always unity, but what is of primary importance is to know the modes and forms of the determination of this unity.

Manifestation, development, determination do not go on to infinity, nor yet do they stop accidentally. But in the course of its true development the Notion completes its course by a return upon itself, whereby it has attained the reality adequate to it. So it is that the manifestation is infinite in nature, that the content is adequate to the Notion of spirit, and that the phenomenal world exists, like spirit, in and for itself.

In religion, the Notion of religion has become its own object. Spirit which is in and for itself has now no longer in its development individual forms and determinations, it knows itself no longer as spirit in such determinability or such a limited moment; but it has triumphed over these limitations and this finiteness, and is for itself that which also it is in itself. This cognisance in which spirit is for itself what it is in itself constitutes the in-and-for of spirit which is in possession of knowledge, the perfect and absolute religion, in which is revealed what spirit is, what God is. That is the Christian religion.

ARTHUR SCHOPENHAUER

(1788-1860)

"We should be greatly and childishly mistaken if we thought that all the just and lawful acts of mankind had a moral origin."

Most philosophers in the western tradition tend toward optimism, believing in the possibility of human improvement, individual and societal. A great exception is Arthur Schopenhauer, the nineteenth century German pessimist, whose concept of the mindless, life-governing will to live underlies his insistence that selfishness dominates human affairs.

In Schopenhauer's major work, *The World as Will and Idea* (1819), he established and developed his basic ideas, but to the chagrin of the young scholar, his ambitious work was largely ignored. Later in his life he came to be more understood and appreciated, and the publication of Darwin's theories on evolution gave some scientific authority to his observations about the struggle that defines existence.

The following passage from Schopenhauer's 1841 essay "On the Basis of Morality" draws out some of the moral implications of the innate egoism which, according to the author, lies behind almost all human behavior.

ON THE BASIS OF MORALITY

ARTHUR SCHOPENHAUER

Skeptical View

Might it not follow from a retrospective glance at the vain attempts to find a sure basis of morals for more than two thousand years that there is no natural morality at all that is independent of human institution? On the contrary, might it not be inferred that this is nothing but an artificial product, a means invented for the better restraint of the selfish and wicked human race, and that accordingly, without the support of positive religions, it would fail, since it had no internal credentials and no natural basis? Justice and the police cannot suffice everywhere, for there are offenses whose discovery is too difficult; indeed, the punishment of some of them, where we are left without public protection, is a precious business. Moreover, civil law can at the very most enforce justice, but not philanthropy and beneficence, since here everyone would like to be the passive part and no one the active. This has given rise to the hypothesis that morality rests solely on religion, and that both have the same aim of being the complement to the necessary inadequacy of legislation and the machinery of State. Accordingly it is said that there cannot be a natural morality, in other words, one based merely on the nature of things or of man, and that this explains why philosophers have looked in vain for its foundation. This opinion is not without plausibility, and was already advanced by the Pyrrhonians: "By nature there is nothing either good or bad; but human opinion has made the difference; as Timon says." Also in modern times distinguished thinkers have professed it. It therefore merits careful examination, although being more conveniently shelved by an inquisitorial side glance at the conscience of those conceiving such an idea.

We should be greatly and childishly mistaken if we thought that all the just and lawful acts of mankind had a moral origin. On the contrary, the relation between justice as practiced by men and genuine honesty of heart is analogous to that between the expressions of politeness and the genuine love for one's neighbor. Unlike politeness, such love overcomes egoism not ostensibly, but actually. We see everywhere paraded an honesty of sentiment that tries to be beyond any doubt, and a deep indignation, ready to turn to the most furious anger, roused at the slightest hint of a suspicion in this direction. But only the inexperienced simpleton will take all this for pure coin and for the effect of a tender moral feeling or conscience. In reality, universal honesty and uprightness, as practiced in human intercourse and affirmed in the most unshaken maxims, rest mainly on two external necessities: first, on the order of the law whereby everyone's rights are protected by public authority, and secondly, on the recognized necessity of a good name or civil honor for making one's way in the world. By their means everyone's steps are under the supervision of public opinion, which is inexorably severe, and in this respect never forgives even a single false step, but remembers it as an indelible stain on the guilty man for the rest of his life. Here public opinion is really wise, for it starts from the fundamental principle, "What we do follows from what we are," and, accordingly, from the conviction that the character is unalterable and that what a man has *once* done he will inevitably do again in precisely the same circumstances. These then are the two guardians that watch over public honesty, and without which we should be in a bad way, to speak frankly, particularly as regards property, this central point in human life on which life's energy and activity mainly turn. For assuming that purely ethical motives to honesty and integrity exist, they can for the most part be applied to civil possessions only in a very roundabout way. Thus, they can relate primarily and directly only to *natural* right, but to *positive* right only indirectly, namely, insofar as the latter is based on the former. But natural right attaches to no other property than that which a man has acquired through his own exertions; and when this is seized, the owner is at the same time deprived of the efforts expended by him in acquiring it. (I reject absolutely the theory of preoccupancy, yet here I cannot go into its refutation.) Now every possession based on positive right should, of course, rest ultimately and in the last instance on the natural right of property, no matter how many intermediate links are involved. But what a distance there is in most cases between our civil possession and that original source of the natural right of property! The connection between them is often very difficult and even impossible to demonstrate. Our property is inherited, acquired through marriage, won at a lottery, or, if not in this way, is still not acquired by our own work, by the sweat of our brow, but rather through cunning thoughts and bright ideas, in speculation with stocks and shares, for example. In fact, it is sometimes acquired through stupid ideas which, by means of chance, have been crowned and glorified by the *Deus eventus*. Only in the smallest number of cases is property really the fruit of actual labor and effort, and even then this work is often only mental, like that of lawyers, doctors, officials, and teachers, and, in the eyes of the crude and uncultured, appears to cost little exertion. It needs considerable culture and education to recognize the ethical right in the case of all such possessions, and accordingly to respect it from a purely moral incentive. Therefore many secretly regard the property of others as being possessed solely in accordance with positive right; and thus if they find the means to wrest it from them by making use of, or even evading, the laws, they have no compunction about doing so. For to them it seems that the others would lose their property in the same way it was previously acquired; and therefore they regard their own claims as being just as well founded as those of the previous owner. From their point of view, the right of the stronger has in civil society been superseded by that of the shrewder. Meanwhile, the *wealthy man* is often of inviolable integrity, because he is wholeheartedly devoted to a rule and maintains a maxim on whose observance depend his entire possessions and the many advantages he thereby enjoys. He is therefore thoroughly in earnest in his profession of the fundamental principle *suum cuique* (to each his own), and never departs from it. There is, in fact, an *objective* devotion to loyalty and good faith, with the resolve to keep them inviolable. Such devotion rests merely on the fact that loyalty and good faith are the basis of all free intercourse among men, of good order and secure possession. They are, therefore, very often of benefit *to ourselves,* and in this respect must be maintained even at some sacrifice, just as we also *expend* something on a good piece of land. Yet honesty established in this way will as a rule be found only among the well-to-do, or at any rate among those who are engaged in a lucrative business. It is met with most of all among merchants, who are most clearly convinced that the indispensable supports of commercial life and activity are mutual trust and credit; and thus commercial honor is in a class by itself. The *poor* man, on the other hand, who has come off badly and, by virtue of an inequality of property, sees himself condemned to want and hard work while others openly and obviously live in luxury and idleness, will hardly acknowledge that underlying this inequality is a corresponding inequality of merit and honest livelihood. But if he does *not* recognize this, then how is he to find the purely ethical impulse to honesty and uprightness which prevents him from reaching for and grasping the superfluous wealth of others? It is generally the order of the law that restrains him. But if ever the rare occasion occurs when he is safe from the effects of the law and can by a single act throw off the oppressive burden of want, which makes itself felt all the more by the sight of another's wealth, and *he* can come into the possession and enjoyment of pleasures so often coveted, what then will restrain his hand? Religious dogmas? Rarely is faith so firm. A purely moral motive to justice and fairness? Perhaps in isolated cases. In the greatest majority, however, it will be only anxiety for his good name, his civil honor, a matter of great importance even to a humble man. It will be the obvious danger of, through such an act, forever being expelled from the great masonic lodge of honorable men who observe the law of uprightness and accordingly have apportioned among themselves and manage property all over the world. In consequence of a single dishonorable act a man runs the risk of being an outcast from civil society for the rest of his life. He will be one whom no one will ever trust again, whose company is shunned by everyone, and from whom all advancement is thus cut off. In other words, he will be branded as "a fellow who has stolen"; to him the proverb applies: "Whoever once steals is all his life a thief."

These, then, are the guardians of public honesty, and whoever has lived and kept his eyes open will admit that by far the greatest number of honorable actions in human intercourse is to be attributed to them alone. In fact, he will have to admit that there are not wanting men who hope to elude even *their* vigilance, and who therefore regard justice and honesty merely as a signboard, a banner, under whose protection they practice their piracy the more successfully. Thus, we should not at once fly into holy wrath and buckle on our armor if a moralist raises the problem of whether all justice and honesty are at bottom perhaps merely conventional. We must not be indignant if the moralist continues to pursue this principle and endeavors to trace all the rest of morality to more remote, indirect, but ultimately egoistic grounds, as was cleverly and ingeniously attempted by Holbach, Helvétius, d'Alembert, and others of their time. This is even actually true and correct of the greatest number of just actions, as I have already shown. There can be no doubt that it is also true of a considerable number of actions of philanthropy; for they often result from ostentation, very frequently from a belief in a retribution to come which might be carried out in the second, or wholly in the third degree, or they admit even of other egoistic grounds. But it is just as certain that there are actions of disinterested philanthropy and of entirely voluntary justice. To appeal not to the facts of consciousness, but simply to experience, I refer to isolated, yet indubitable cases as proofs of such actions. Not only was the danger of legal prosecution entirely excluded here, but that of discovery and even of suspicion, and yet the rich man was given his property by the poor: for instance, something is lost, found, and returned to the owner; a deposit made by a third party, who has since died, is restored to the rightful owner; a sum of money is privately entrusted to a poor man by a fugitive for whom it is faithfully kept and to whom it is returned. Undoubtedly there are cases of this kind, but the surprise, the deep emotion, and the high respect with which we welcome them are clear evidence that they belong to the things we do not expect, and are rare exceptions. Indeed, there are really honest people just as there are actually four-leaved clover; but Hamlet does not exaggerate when he says, "To be honest, as this world goes, is to be one man pick'd out of ten thousand." It may be objected that ultimately religious dogmas, and thus regard for punishment and reward in another world, underlie the above-mentioned actions; but against this, cases could perhaps be indicated wherein the performers of such actions belonged to no religious faith at all. This is by no means as rare as people profess.

In face of the *skeptical view,* appeal is made in the first instance to *conscience;* but doubts are raised even against its natural origin. At any rate, there is also a *spurious conscience* that is often confused with the genuine. The remorse and anxiety that are felt by many a man for what he has done are often basically nothing but the fear of what may happen to him. The violation of external, arbitrary, and even absurd rules torments many a man with inner reproaches precisely as does conscience. Thus, for example, many a bigoted Jew is actually oppressed by the thought that, although it says in Exodus 35:3, "Ye shall kindle no fire throughout your habitations upon the sabbath day," he nevertheless smoked a pipe at home on Saturday. Many a nobleman or officer is stung by secret self-reproach because, in the case of some rebuke, he did not properly comply with the laws of the fools' code called knightly honor. This can go to such lengths that many a man of this class will blow out his brains if he finds it impossible to keep his word of honor, or even to do enough for the aforesaid code in the case of quarrels and disputes. (Instances of both have come to my knowledge.) On the other hand, the same man will any day lightheartedly break his promise if only the shibboleth "honor" is not added. Generally speaking, every inconsistency, every thoughtless action, every action contrary to our resolutions, principles, or convictions, whatever the nature of these; indeed, every indiscretion, every mistake, every stupid blunder, afterward secretly annoys us, and leaves behind a sting in our hearts. Many a man would be astonished if he saw how his conscience, which seems to him such an imposing affair, is really made up. It probably consists of one-fifth fear of men, one-fifth fear of the gods, one-fifth prejudice, one-fifth vanity, and one-fifth habit; so that he is essentially no better than the Englishman who said quite frankly, "I cannot afford to keep a conscience." Religious people of every faith frequently understand by *conscience* nothing but the dogmas and commandments of their religion and the self-scrutiny undertaken with reference to them. In fact, the expressions *coercion of conscience* and *liberty of conscience* are also taken in this sense. The same interpretation was also given by the theologians, schoolmen, and casuists of the Middle Ages and later times; all that a man knew about the rules and precepts of the Church, together with the resolve to believe and observe this, constituted his *conscience*. Accordingly, there were a doubting conscience, an asserting conscience, an erring conscience, and so on, and for their correction a council of conscience was held. We can see briefly from Stäudlin's *History of the Theory of Conscience* [*Geschichte der Lehr vom Gewissen*] how little the concept of conscience, like others, is fixed by its own object, how differently it has been interpreted by different men, how indefinite and uncertain it appears in the works of authors. All these are not calculated to establish the reality of the concepts, and consequently have given rise to the question whether there really is a genuine inborn conscience. In § 10, when dealing with the theory of freedom, I had occasion to state briefly my conception of conscience, and to this I shall later return.

All these skeptical objections taken together certainly do not suffice to deny the existence of all genuine morality, but to moderate our expectations of the moral tendency in man and consequently of the natural foundation of ethics. For much that is ascribed to this foundation can be shown to spring from other motives; and a consideration of the moral depravity of the world proves clearly enough that the incentive to do good cannot be very powerful, especially as it often does not work even where the motives opposing it are not strong; although the individual difference of characters here asserts its full force. Meanwhile, a knowledge of that moral depravity is rendered more difficult by the fact that its manifestations are curbed and concealed by order of the law, by the necessity of honor, and even by politeness. Finally, there is the fact that in education people imagine they promote the morality of the young by representing uprightness and virtue as the maxims that are universally observed in the world. Now if later experience teaches them something different, often to their great detriment, the discovery that the teachers of their youth were the first to deceive them can have a more injurious effect on their own morality than if those teachers themselves had given the first example of frankness and honesty, and had said openly, "The world is sunk in evil, and men are not what they ought to be; do not let that lead you astray, and see that you are better." All this, as I have said, makes it more difficult for us to recognize the actual immorality of the human race. The State, this masterpiece of the rational and accumulated egoism of all which understands itself, has put the protection of everyone's rights into the hands of a power infinitely superior to that of the individual, and compels him to respect the rights of everyone else. The boundless egoism of almost everyone, the wickedness of many, and the cruelty of not a few are then unable to make their appearance; compulsion and coercion have bridled and restrained everyone. The deception springing from this restraint is so great that when in isolated cases where the power of the State cannot protect or is eluded and we plainly see the insatiable greed, the infamous cupidity and mania for money, the deeply concealed perfidy and duplicity, and the spiteful wickedness of men and women, we often recoil with horror, raise an outcry, imagine we have chanced upon a monster never before seen; yet, without the compulsion of laws and the necessity of civil honor, such occurrences would certainly be the order of the day. We have to read criminal narratives and descriptions of the conditions of anarchy if we want to know what man really is from a moral point of view. The thousands who throng before our eyes in peaceful intercourse are to be regarded as just as many tigers and wolves whose teeth are secured by a strong muzzle. Therefore, if one imagines the power of the State as abolished, in other words, the muzzle as cast off, every thinking man will recoil at the expected scene, and in this way, he will show us what little confidence he really has in the efficacy of religion, conscience, or the natural foundation of morals, whatever this may be. But in the face of those unshackled immoral forces, it is then that the true moral incentive in man would openly reveal its efficacy and could in consequence be most easily recognized. At the same time, the incredibly great moral difference in characters would be disclosed and found to be just as great as the intellectual difference in minds, which is certainly saying much.

I shall probably be told that ethics is not concerned with how people actually behave, but that it is the science that states how they *ought* to behave. But this is the very principle which I deny, after showing clearly enough in the critical part of this essay that the concept of *ought*, the *imperative form* of ethics, applies solely to theological morality, and that outside this it loses all sense and meaning. I assume, on the other hand, that the purpose of ethics is to indicate, explain, and trace to its ultimate ground the extremely varied behavior of men from a moral point of view. Therefore there is no other way of discovering the foundation of ethics than the empirical, namely, to investigate whether there are generally any actions to which we must attribute *genuine moral worth*. Such will be actions of voluntary justice, pure philanthropy, and real magnanimity. These are then to be regarded as a given phenomenon that we have to explain correctly, that is, trace to its true grounds. Consequently, we have to indicate the peculiar motive that moves man to actions of this kind, a kind specifically different from any other. This motive together with the susceptibility to it will be the ultimate ground of morality, and a knowledge of it will be the foundation of morals. This is the humble path to which I direct ethics; it contains no construction a priori, no absolute legislation for all rational beings *in abstracto*. Whoever thinks that it is not sufficiently fashionable, doctrinaire, and academic, may return to the categorical imperatives, to the shibboleth of the "dignity of man," to the hollow phrases, the brain-webs and soap bubbles of the schools, to principles ridiculed at every step by experience, to principles whereof no one outside the lecture halls knows anything or has ever had any experience. On the other hand, the foundation of morals that is reached on my path is upheld by experience, which daily and hourly affords its silent testimony in favor thereof.

SOREN KIERKEGAARD

(1813-1855)

"But one thing I will not do, not for anything in the world. I will not by suppression, or by performing tricks, try to produce the impression that the ordinary Christianity in the land and the Christianity of the New Testament are alike."

Kierkegaard was ignored by some and derided by others in early nineteenth century Copenhagen. As a thinker who embodied and anticipated the passionate individuality which produced the existentialism of the twentieth century, he was constantly at odds with the conventional outlook of his Danish contemporaries. The passion which Kierkegaard found essential to his faith emerged early in his experience. In *The Journals*, which he began as a young man, he wrote that he must find one "idea for which I can live and die." It is difficult to find in the literature of ideas a body of work so dedicated to such a guiding principle as the vast and varied effort of Kierkegaard.

His insistence on uncompromising commitment to what one believes brought Kierkegaard into conflict with the more comfortable convictions of his time, producing late in his life "The Attack upon Christendom." In this unsettling work Kierkegaard echoes and affirms the words of Jesus: "Narrow is the way...and few are they that find it."

ATTACK ON CHRISTENDOM

SOREN KIEREKEGAARD

Quite simply: I want honesty. I am not, as well-intentioned people represent (for I can pay no attention to the interpretations of me that are advance by exasperation and rage and impotence and twaddle), I am not a Christian severity as opposed to a Christian leniency.

By no means. I am neither leniency nor severity: I am—a human honesty.

The leniency which is the common Christianity in the land I want to place alongside of the New Testament in order to see how these two are related to one another.

Then, if it appears, if I or another can prove, that it can be maintained face to face with the New Testament, then with the greatest joy I will agree to it.

But one thing I will not do, not for anything in the world. I will not by suppression, or by performing tricks, try to produce the impression that the ordinary Christianity in the land and the Christianity of the New Testament are alike.

Behold, this it is I do not want. And why not? Well, because I want honesty. Or, if you wish me to talk in another way—well then, it is because I believe that, if possibly even the very extremest softening down of Christianity may hold good in the judgment of eternity, it is impossible that it should hold good when even artful tricks are employed to gloss over the difference between the Christianity of the New Testament and this softened form. What I mean is this: If a man is known for his graciousness—very well then, let me venture to ask him to forgive me all my debt; but even though his grace were divine grace, this is too much to ask, if I will not even be truthful about how great the debt is.

And this in my opinion is the falsification of which official Christianity is guilty: it does not frankly and unreservedly make known the Christian requirement—perhaps because it is afraid people would shudder to see at what a distance from it we are living, without being able to claim that in the remotest way our life might be called an effort in the direction of fulfilling the requirement. Or (merely to take one example of what is everywhere present in the New Testament): when Christ requires us to save our life eternally (and that surely is what we propose to attain as Christians) and to hate our own life in this world, is there then a single one among us whose life in the remotest degree could be called even the weakest effort in this direction? And perhaps there are thousands of "Christians" in the land who are not so much as aware of this requirement. So then we "Christians" are living, and are loving our life, just in the ordinary human sense. If then by "grace" God will nevertheless regard us as Christians, one thing at least must be required: that we, being precisely aware of the requirement, have a true conception of how infinitely great is the grace that is shown us. "Grace" cannot possibly stretch so far; one thing it must never be used for, it must never be used to suppress or to diminish the requirement; for in that case "grace" would turn Christianity upside down.

Or, to take an example of another kind: A teacher is paid, let us say, several thousand. If then we suppress the Christian standard and apply the ordinary human rule, that it is a matter of course a man should receive a wage for his labor, a wage sufficient to support a family, and a considerable wage to enable him to enjoy the consideration due to a government official—then a few thousand a year is certainly not much. On the other hand, as soon as the Christian requirement of poverty is brought to bear, family is a luxury and several thousand is very high pay. I do not say this in order to deprive such an official of a single shilling, if I were able to; on the contrary, if he desired it, and I were able, he might well have double as many thousands: but I say that the suppression of the Christian requirement changes the point of view for all his wages. Honesty to Christianity demands that one call to mind the Christian requirement of poverty, which is not a capricious whim of Christianity, but is because only in poverty can it be truly served, and the more thousands a teacher of Christianity has by way of wages, the less he can serve Christianity. On the other hand, it is not honest to suppress the requirement or to perform artful tricks to produce the impression that this sort of business career is simply the Christianity of the New Testament. No—let us take money, but for God's sake not the next thing: let us not wish to gloss over the Christian requirement, so that by suppression or by falsification we may bring about an appearance of decorum which is in the very highest degree demoralizing and is a sly death-blow to Christianity.

Therefore I want honesty; but still now the Established Church has not been willing of its own accord to go in for that sort of honesty, and neither has it been willing to let itself be influenced by me. That does not make me, however, a leniency or a severity; no, I am and remain quite simply a human honesty.

The Comfortable — and the Concern for an Eternal Blessedness

It is these two things—one might also be tempted to say, what the deuce have these two things to do with one another?—and yet it is these two things that official Christianity, or the State by the aid of official Christianity, has jumbled together, and done it as calmly as when, at a party where the host wants to include everybody, he jumbles many toasts in one.

It seems that the reasoning of the State must have been as follows. Among the many various things which man needs on a civilized plan and which the State tries to provide for its citizens as cheaply and comfortable as possible—among these very various things, like public security, water, illumination, roads, bridge-building, etc., etc., there is also—an eternal blessedness in the hereafter, a requirement which the State ought also to satisfy (how generous of it!), and that in as cheap and comfortable a way as possible. Of course it will cost money, for without money one gets nothing in this world, not even a certificate of eternal blessedness in the other world; no, without money one gets nothing in this world. Yet all the same, what the State does, to the great advantage of the individual, is that one gets it from the State at a cheaper price than if the individual were to make some private arrangement, moreover it is more secure, and finally it is comfortable in a degree that only can be provided on a big scale. . . .

Far be it from me to speak disparagingly of the comfortable! Let it be applied wherever it can be applied, in relation to everything which is in such a sense a thing that this thing can be possessed irrespective of the way in which it is possessed, so that one can have it either in this way or in the other; for when such is the case, the convenient and comfortable way is undeniably to be preferred. Take water for example: water is a thing which can be procured in the difficult way of fetching it up from the pump, but it can also be procured in the convenient way of high pressure; naturally I prefer the more convenient way.

But the eternal is not a thing which can be had regardless of the way in which it is acquired. The eternal is acquired in *one* way, and the eternal is different from everything else precisely for the fact that it can be acquired only in one single way; conversely, what can be acquired in only one way is the eternal—it is acquired only in one way, in the difficult way which Christ indicated by the words: "Narrow is the gate and straitened the way that leadeth unto life, and few are they that find it."

That was bad news! The comfortable—precisely the thing in which our age excels—absolutely cannot be applied with respect to an eternal blessedness. When, for example, the thing you are required to do is to walk, it is no use at all to make the most astonishing inventions in the way of the easiest carriages and to want to covey yourself in these when the task prescribed to you was—walking. And if the eternal is the way in which it is acquired, it doesn't do any good to want to alter this way, however admirably, in the direction of comfort; for the eternal is acquired only in the difficult way, is not acquired indifferently both in the easy and the difficult way, but is the way in which it is acquired, and this way is the difficult one. . . .

A Eulogy upon the Human Race or A Proof That the New Testament Is No Longer Truth

In the New Testament the Saviour of the world, our Lord Jesus Christ, represents the situation thus: The way that leadeth unto life is straitened, the gate narrow—few be they that find it!

—Now, on the contrary, to speak only of Denmark, we are all Christians, the way is as broad as it possibly can be, the broadest in Denmark, since it is the way in which we all are walking, besides being in all respects as convenient, as comfortable as possible; and the gate is as wide as it possibly can be, wider surely a gate cannot be than that through which we all are going *en masse*.

Ergo the New Testament is no longer truth

All honor to the human race! But Thou, O Saviour of the world, Thou didst entertain too lowly a notion of the human race, failing to foresee the sublime heights to which, perfectible as it is, it can attain by an effort steadily pursued!

To that degree therefore the New Testament is not longer truth: the way the broadest, the gate the widest, and all of us Christians. Yea, I venture to go a step further—it inspires me with enthusiasm, for this, you must remember, is a eulogy upon the human race—I venture to maintain that, on the average, the Jews who dwell among us are to a certain degree Christians, Christians like all the others—to that degree we are all Christians, in that degree is the New Testament no longer truth. . . . I venture to go a step further, without expressing, however, any definite opinion, seeing that in this respect I lack precise information, and hence submit to persons well informed, the specialists, the question whether among the domestic animals, the nobler ones, the horse, the dog, the cow, there might not be visible some Christian token. That is not unlikely. Just think what it means to live in a Christian state, a Christian nation, where everything is Christian, and we are all Christians, where, however a man twists and turns, he sees nothing but Christianity and Christendom, the truth and witnesses to the truth—it is not unlikely that this may have an influence upon the nobler domestic animals, and thereby in turn upon that which, according to the judgment of both the veterinary and the priest, is the most important thing, namely, the progeny. Jacob's cunning device is well known, how in order to get speckled lambs he laid speckled rods in the watering troughs, so that the ewes saw nothing but speckles and therefore gave birth to speckled lambs. It is not unlikely—although I do not presume to have any definite opinion, as I am not a specialist, and therefore would rather submit the question to a committee composed, for example, of veterinaries and priests—it is not unlikely that it will end with domestic animals in "Christendom" bringing into the world a Christian progeny.

I am almost dizzy at the thought; but then, on the greatest possible scale—to the honor of the human race—will the New Testament be no longer truth.

Thou Saviour of the world, Thou didst anxiously exclaim, "When I come again, shall I find faith on the earth?" and then didst bow Thy head in death; Thou surely didst not have the least idea that in such a measure Thine expectations would be surpassed, that the human race in such a pretty and touching way would make the New Testament untruth and Thine importance almost doubtful. For can such good beings truthfully be said to need, or ever to have needed, a saviour?

JOHN STUART MILL

(1806-1873)

"It is better to be a human being dissatisfied than a pig satisfied; better to be Socrates dissatisfied than a fool satisfied. And if the fool, or the pig, are of a different opinion, it is because they only know their own side of the question. The other party to the comparison knows both sides."

Although Jeremy Bentham first voiced in England the political and philosophical principles that came to be known as Utilitarianism, it was John Stuart Mill, encouraged by his father James, who became the foremost spokesman for the radical social view that championed "the greatest good for the greatest number."

Utilitarian thinkers, as emphasized by Mill in the following excerpt, traced the origin of their moral system to Epicurus, but Mill's formulation of the philosophy departs from the Greek's traditional hedonism on two important points. Mill argues that some pleasures, are superior to others intrinsically, as well as circumstantially. He also observes that the pursuit of pleasure has ennobling consequences, evolving from egoism to altruism.

UTILITARIANISM

JOHN STUART MILL

What Utilitarianism Is

The creed which accepts as the foundation of morals "utility" or the "greatest happiness principle" holds that actions are right in proportion as they tend to promote happiness; wrong as they tend to produce the reverse of happiness. By happiness is intended pleasure and the absence of pain; by unhappiness, pain and the privation of pleasure. To give a clear view of the moral standard set up by the theory, much more requires to be said; in particular, what things it includes in the ideas of pain and pleasure, and to what extent this is left an open question. But these supplementary explanations do not affect the theory of life on which this theory of morality is grounded—namely, that pleasure and freedom from pain are the only things desirable as ends; and that all desirable things (which are as numerous in the utilitarian as in any other scheme) are desirable either for pleasure inherent in themselves or as means to the promotion of pleasure and the prevention of pain.

Now such a theory of life excites in many minds, and among them in some of the most estimable in feeling and purpose, inveterate dislike. To suppose that life has (as they express it) no higher end than pleasure—no better and nobler object of desire and pursuit—they designate as utterly mean and groveling, as a doctrine worthy only of swine, to whom the followers of Epicurus were, at a very early period, contemptuously likened; and modern holders of the doctrine are occasionally made the subject of equally polite comparisons by its German, French, and English assailants.

When thus attacked, the Epicureans have always answered that it is not they, but their accusers, who represent human nature in a degrading light, since the accusation supposes human beings to be capable of no pleasures except those of which swine are capable. If this supposition were true, the charge could not be gainsaid, but would then be no longer an imputation; for if the sources of pleasure were precisely the same to human beings and to swine, the rule of life which is good enough for the one would be good enough for the other. The comparison of the Epicurean life to that of beasts is felt as degrading, precisely because a beast's pleasures do not satisfy a human being's conceptions of happiness. Human beings have faculties more elevated than the animal appetites and, when once made conscious of them, do not regard anything as happiness which does not include their gratification. I do not, indeed, consider the Epicureans to have been by any means faultless in drawing out their scheme of consequences from the utilitarian principle. To do this in any sufficient manner, many Stoic, as well as Christian, elements require to be included. But there is no known Epicurean theory of life which does not assign to the pleasures of the intellect, of the feelings and imagination, and of the moral sentiments a much higher value as pleasures than to those of mere sensation. It must be admitted, however, that utilitarian writers in general have placed the superiority of mental over bodily pleasures chiefly in the greater permanency, safety, uncostliness, etc., of the former—that is, in their circumstantial advantages rather than in their intrinsic nature. And on all these points utilitarians have fully proved their case; but they might have taken the other and, as it may be called, higher ground with entire consistency. It is quite compatible with the principle of utility to recognize the fact that some kinds of pleasure are more desirable and more valuable than others. It would be absurd that, while in estimating all other things quality is considered as well as quantity, the estimation of pleasure should be supposed to depend on quantity alone.

If I am asked what I mean by difference of quality in pleasures, or what makes one pleasure more valuable than another, merely as a pleasure, except its being greater in amount, there is but one possible answer. Of two pleasures, if there be one to which all or almost all who have experience of both give a decided preference, irrespective of any feeling of moral obligation to prefer it, that is the more desirable pleasure. If one of the two is, by those who are competently acquainted with both, placed so far above the other that they prefer it, even though knowing it to be attended with a greater amount of discontent, and would not resign it for any quantity of the other pleasure which their nature is capable of, we are justified in ascribing to the preferred enjoyment a superiority in quality so far outweighing quantity as to render it, in comparison, of small account.

Now it is an unquestionable fact that those who are equally acquainted with and equally capable of appreciating and enjoying both do give a most marked preference to the manner of existence which employs their higher faculties. Few human creatures would consent to be changed into any of the lower animals for a promise of the fullest allowance of a beast's pleasures; no intelligent human being would consent to be a fool, no instructed person would be an ignoramus, no person of feeling and conscience would be selfish and base, even though they should be persuaded that the fool, the dunce, or the rascal is better satisfied with his lot than they are with theirs. They would not resign what they possess more than he for the most complete satisfaction of all the desires which they have in common with him. If they ever fancy they would, it is only in cases of unhappiness so extreme that to escape from it they would exchange their lot for almost any other, however undesirable in their own eyes. A being of higher faculties requires more to make him happy, is capable probably of more acute suffering, and certainly accessible to it at more points, than one of an inferior type; but in spite of these liabilities, he can never really wish to sink into what he feels to be a lower grade of existence. We may give what explanation we please of this unwillingness; we may attribute it to pride, a name which is given indiscriminately to some of the most and to some of the least estimable feelings of which mankind are capable; we may refer it to the love of liberty and personal independence, an appeal to which was with the Stoics one of the most effective means for the inculcation of it; to the love of power or to the love of excitement, both of which do really enter into and contribute to it; but its most appropriate appellation is a sense of dignity, which all human beings possess in one form or other, and in some, though by no means in exact, proportion to their higher faculties, and which is so essential a part of the happiness of those in whom it is strong that nothing which conflicts with it could be otherwise than momentarily an object of desire to them. Whoever supposes that this preference takes place at a sacrifice of happiness—that the superior being, in anything like equal circumstances, is not happier than the inferior—confounds the two very different ideas of happiness and content. It is indisputable that the being whose capacities of enjoyment are low has the greatest chance of having them fully satisfied; and a highly endowed being will always feel that any happiness which he can look for, as the world is constituted, is imperfect. But he can learn to bear its imperfections, if they are at all bearable; and they will not make him envy the being who is indeed unconscious of the imperfections, but only because he feels not at all the good which those imperfections qualify. It is better to be a human being dissatisfied than a pig satisfied; better to be Socrates dissatisfied than a fool satisfied. And if the fool, or the pig, are of a different opinion, it is because they only know their own side of the question. The other party to the comparison knows both sides.

It may be objected that many who are capable of the higher pleasures occasionally, under the influence of temptation, postpone them to the lower. But this is quite compatible with a full appreciation of the intrinsic superiority of the higher. Men often, from infirmity of character, make their election for the nearer good, though they know it to be the less valuable; and this no less when the choice is between two bodily pleasures than when it is between bodily and mental. They pursue sensual indulgences to the injury of health, though perfectly aware that health is the greater good. It may be further objected that many who begin with youthful enthusiasm for everything noble, as they advance in years, sink into indolence and selfishness. But I do not believe that those who undergo this very common change voluntarily choose the lower description of pleasures in preference to the higher. I believe that, before they devote themselves exclusively to the one, they have already become incapable of the other. Capacity for the nobler feelings is in most natures a very tender plant, easily killed, not only by hostile influences, but by mere want of sustenance; and in the majority of young persons it speedily dies away if the occupations to which their position in life has devoted them, and the society into which it has thrown them, are not favorable to keeping that higher capacity in exercise. Men lose their high aspirations as they lose their intellectual tastes, because they have not time or opportunity for indulging them; and they addict themselves to inferior pleasures, not because they deliberately prefer them, but because they are either the only ones to which they have access or the only ones which they are any longer capable of enjoying. It may be questioned whether anyone who has remained equally susceptible to both classes of pleasures ever knowingly and calmly preferred the lower, though many, in all ages, have broken down in an ineffectual attempt to combine both.

From this verdict of the only competent judges, I apprehend there can be no appeal. On a question which is the best worth having of two pleasures, or which of two modes of existence is the most grateful to the feelings, apart from its moral attributes and from its consequences, the judgment of those who are qualified by knowledge of both, or, if they differ, that of the majority among them, must be admitted as final. And there needs be the less hesitation to accept this judgment respecting the quality of pleasures, since there is no other tribunal to be referred to even on the question of quantity. What means are there of determining which is the acutest of two pains, or the intensest of two pleasurable sensations, except the general suffrage of those who are familiar with both? Neither pains nor pleasures are homogeneous, and pain is always heterogeneous with pleasure. What is there to decide whether a particular pleasure is worth purchasing at the cost of a particular pain, except the feelings and judgment of the experienced? When, therefore, those feelings and judgment declare the pleasures derived from the higher faculties to be preferable *in kind,* apart from the question of intensity, to those of which the animal nature, disjoined from the higher faculties, is susceptible, they are entitled on this subject to the same regard.

I have dwelt on this point as being a necessary part of a perfectly just conception of utility or happiness considered as the directive rule of human conduct. But it is by no means an indispensable condition to the acceptance of the utilitarian standard; for that standard is not the agent's own greatest happiness, but the greatest amount of happiness altogether; and if it may possibly be doubted whether a noble character is always the happier for its nobleness, there can be no doubt that it makes other people happier, and that the world in general is immensely a gainer by it. Utilitarianism, therefore, could only attain its end by the general cultivation of nobleness of character, even if each individual were only benefited by the nobleness of others, and his own, so far as happiness is concerned, were a sheer deduction from the benefit. But the bare enunciation of such an absurdity as this last renders refutation superfluous.

According to the greatest happiness principle, as above explained, the ultimate end, with reference to and for the sake of which all other things are desirable—whether we are considering our own good or that of other people—is an existence exempt as far as possible from pain, and as rich as possible in enjoyments, both in point of quantity and quality; the test of quality and the rule for measuring it against quantity being the preference felt by those who, in their opportunities of experience, to which must be added their habits of self-consciousness and self-observation, are best furnished with the means of comparison. This, being according to the utilitarian opinion the end of human action, is necessarily also the standard of morality, which may accordingly be defined "the rules and precepts for human conduct," by the observance of which an existence such as has been described might be, to the greatest extent possible, secured to all mankind; and not to them only, but, so far as the nature of things admits, to the whole sentient creation.

Against this doctrine, however, arises another class of objectors who say that happiness, in any form, cannot be the rational purpose of human life and action; because, in the first place, it is unattainable; and they contemptuously ask, What right hast thou to be happy?—a question which Mr. Carlyle clinches by the addition, What right, a short time ago, hadst thou even *to be?* Next they say that men can do *without* happiness; that all noble human beings have felt this, and could not have become noble but by learning the lesson of *Entsagen,* or renunciation: which lesson, thoroughly learned and submitted to, they affirm to be the beginning and necessary condition of all virtue.

The first of these objections would go to the root of the matter were it well founded; for if no happiness is to be had at all by human beings, the attainment of it cannot be the end of morality or of any rational conduct. Though, even in that case, something might still be said for the utilitarian theory, since utility includes not solely the pursuit of happiness, but the prevention or mitigation of unhappiness; and if the former aim be chimerical, there will be all the greater scope and more imperative need for the latter, so long at least as mankind think fit to live and do not take refuge in the simultaneous act of suicide recommended under certain conditions by Novalis. When, however, it is thus positively asserted to be impossible that human life should be happy, the assertion, if not something like a verbal quibble, is at least an exaggeration. If by happiness be meant a continuity of highly pleasurable excitement, it is evident enough that this is impossible. A state of exalted pleasure lasts only moments or in some cases, and with some intermissions, hours or days, and is the occasional brilliant flash of enjoyment, not its permanent and steady flame. Of this the philosophers who have taught that happiness is the end of life were as fully aware as those who taunt them. The happiness which they meant was not a life of rapture, but moments of such, in an existence made up of few and transitory pains, many and various pleasures, with a decided predominance of the active over the passive, and having as the foundation of the whole not to expect more from life than it is capable of bestowing. A life thus composed, to those who have been fortunate enough to obtain it, has always appeared worthy of the name of happiness. And such an existence is even now the lot of many during some considerable portion of their lives. The present wretched education and wretched social arrangements are the only hindrance to its being attainable by almost all.

The objectors perhaps may doubt whether human beings, if taught to consider happiness as the end of life, would be satisfied with such a moderate share of it. But great numbers of mankind have been satisfied with much less. The main constituents of a satisfied life appear to be two, either of which by itself is often found sufficient for the purpose: tranquility and excitement. With such tranquility, many find that they can be content with very little pleasure; with much excitement, many can reconcile themselves to a considerable quantity of pain. There is assuredly no inherent impossibility of enabling even the mass of mankind to unite both, since the two are so far from being incompatible that they are in natural alliance, the prolongation of either being a preparation for, and exciting a wish for, the other. It is only those in whom indolence amounts to a vice that do not desire excitement after an interval of repose; it is only those in whom the need of excitement is a disease that feel the tranquility which follows excitement dull and insipid, instead of pleasurable in direct proportion to the excitement which preceded it. When people who are tolerably fortunate in their outward lot do not find in life sufficient enjoyment to make it valuable to them, the cause generally is caring for nobody but themselves. To those who have neither public nor private affections, the excitements of life are much curtailed, and in any case dwindle in value as the time approaches when all selfish interests must be terminated by death; while those who leave after them objects of personal affection, and especially those who have also cultivated a fellow-feeling with the collective interests of mankind, retain as lively an interest in life on the eve of death as in the vigor of youth and health. Next to selfishness, the principal cause which makes life unsatisfactory is want of mental cultivation. A cultivated mind—I do not mean that of a philosopher, but any mind to which the fountains of knowledge have been opened, and which has been taught, in any tolerable degree, to exercise its faculties—finds sources of inexhaustible interest in all that surrounds it: in the objects of nature, the achievements of art, the imaginations of poetry, the incidents of history, the ways of mankind, past and present, and their prospects in the future. It is possible, indeed, to become indifferent to all this, and that too without having exhausted a thousandth part of it, but only when one has had from the beginning no moral or human interest in these things and has sought in them only the gratification of curiosity.

Now there is absolutely no reason in the nature of things why an amount of mental culture sufficient to give an intelligent interest in these objects of contemplation should not be the inheritance of everyone born in a civilized country. As little is there an inherent necessity that any human being should be a selfish egotist, devoid of every feeling or care but those which center in his own miserable individuality. Something far superior to this is sufficiently common even now, to give ample earnest of what the human species may be made. Genuine private affections and a sincere interest in the public good are possible, though in unequal degrees, to every rightly brought up human being. In a world in which there is so much to interest, so much to enjoy, and so much also to correct and improve, everyone who has this moderate amount of moral and intellectual requisites is capable of an existence which may be called enviable; and unless such a person, through bad laws or subjection to the will of others, is denied the liberty to use the sources of happiness within his reach, he will not fail to find this enviable existence, if he escape the positive evils of life, the great sources of physical and mental suffering—such as indigence, disease, and the unkindness, worthlessness, or premature loss of objects of affection. The main stress of the problem lies, therefore, in the contest with these calamities from which it is a rare good fortune entirely to escape; which, as things now are, cannot be obviated, and often cannot be in any material degree mitigated. Yet no one whose opinion deserves a moment's consideration can doubt that most of the great positive evils of the world are in themselves removable, and will, if human affairs continue to improve, be in the end reduced within narrow limits. Poverty, in any sense implying suffering, may be completely extinguished by the wisdom of society combined with the good sense and providence of individuals. Even that most intractable of enemies, disease, may be indefinitely reduced in dimensions by good physical and moral education and proper control of noxious influences, while the progress of science holds out a promise for the future of still more direct conquests over this detestable foe. And every advance in that direction relieves us from some, not only of the chances which cut short our own lives, but, what concerns us still more, which deprive us of those in whom our happiness is wrapt up. As for vicissitudes of fortune and other disappointments connected with worldly circumstances, these are principally the effect either of gross imprudence, of ill-regulated desires, or of bad or imperfect social institutions. All the grand sources, in short, of human suffering are in a great degree, many of them almost entirely, conquerable by human care and effort; and though their removal is grievously slow—though a long succession of generations will perish in the breach before the conquest is completed, and this world becomes all that, if will and knowledge were not wanting, it might easily be made—yet every mind sufficiently intelligent and generous to bear a part, however small and inconspicuous, in the endeavor will draw a noble enjoyment from the contest itself, which he would not for any bribe in the form of selfish indulgence consent to be without.

FRIEDRICH NIETZSCHE

(1844-1900)

"'Exploitation' does not belong to a depraved, or imperfect and primitive society: it belongs to the nature of the living being as a primary organic function..."

Friedrich Nietzsche was born in the region of Saxony (now part of Germany) in 1844. His father was a Lutheran minister who died when Nietzsche was only five years old. It was intended that young Friedrich was to study theology, but he eventually decided on a career in philology at universities in Bonn and Leipzig. He excelled as a student and was eventually appointed to a prestigious teaching position in Basel. His poor health eventually forced him from the field of teaching. After his teaching career ended, Nietzsche began to write works which place less emphasis on scholarly attainment and more emphasis on his personal philosophy.

One consistent theme in the works of Nietzsche is his challenge to convention. Nietzsche believed that the standards (morals) of society serve only to inhibit personal growth and place mankind into subservient roles. He views traditional philosophy and religion as particularly harmful to humanity. These institutions ask us to take marching orders and place us in the position of being slaves to their rules. *Beyond Good and Evil* consists of a series of critiques of the Western tradition. In this work he challenges us to consider when and why these "rules of society" came about. He urges the individual to create a truth based on self reflection and personal understanding.

Virtually no tradition is spared the wrath of Nietzsche's pen. Despite his early lapse into insanity around 1890, Nietzsche's work has intrigued virtually every generation that has come after him. He has been called "the philosopher" for the twentieth century.

BEYOND GOOD AND EVIL

FRIEDRICH NIETZSCHE

Every elevation of the type "man," has hitherto been the work of an aristocratic society and so it will always be—a society believing in a long scale of gradations of rank and differences of worth among human beings, and requiring slavery in some form or other. Without the *pathos of distance,* such as grows out of the incarnated difference of classes, out of the constant outlooking and downlooking of the ruling caste on subordinates and instruments, and out of their equally constant practice of obeying and commanding, of keeping down and keeping at a distance—that other more mysterious pathos could never have arisen, the longing for an ever new widening of distance within the soul itself, the formation of ever higher, rarer, further, more extended, more comprehensive states, in short, just the elevation of the type "man," the continued "self-surmounting of man," to use a moral formula in a supermoral sense. To be sure, one must not resign oneself to any humanitarian illusions about the history of the origin of an aristocratic society (that is to say, of the preliminary condition for the elevation of the type "man"): the truth is hard. Let us acknowledge unprejudicedly how every higher civilisation hitherto has *originated!* Men with a still natural nature, barbarians in every terrible sense of the word, men of prey, still in possession of unbroken strength of will and desire for power, threw themselves upon weaker, more moral, more peaceful races (perhaps trading or cattle-rearing communities), or upon old mellow civilisations in which the final vital force was flickering out in brilliant fireworks of wit and depravity. At the commencement, the noble caste was always the barbarian caste: their superiority did not consist first of all in their physical, but in their psychical power—they were more *complete* men (which at every point also implies the same as "more complete beasts).

Corruption—as the indication that anarchy threatens to break out among the instincts, and that the foundation of the emotion, called "life," is convulsed—is something radically different according to the organisation in which it manifests itself. When, for instance, an aristocracy like that of France at the beginning of the Revolution, flung away its privileges with sublime disgust and sacrificed itself to an excess of its moral sentiments, it was corruption:—it was really only the closing act of the corruption which had existed for centuries, by virtue of which that aristocracy had abdicated step by step its lordly prerogatives and lowered itself to a *function* of royalty (in the end even to its decoration and parade-dress). The essential thing, however, in a good and healthy aristocracy is that it should *not* regard itself as a function either of the kingship or the commonwealth, but as the *significance* and highest justification thereof—that it should therefore accept with a good conscience the sacrifice of a legion of individuals, who, *for its sake,* must be suppressed and reduced to imperfect men, to slaves and instruments. Its fundamental belief must be precisely that society is *not* allowed to exist for its own sake, but only as a foundation and scaffolding, by means of which a select class of beings may be able to elevate themselves to their higher duties, and in general to a higher *existence*: like those sun-seeking climbing plants in Java—they are called *Sipo Matador,*—which encircle an oak so long and so often with their arms, until at last, high above it, but supported by it, they can unfold their tops in the open light, and exhibit their happiness.

To refrain mutually from injury, from violence, from exploitation, and put one's will on a par with that of others: this may result in a certain rough sense in good conduct among individuals when the necessary conditions are given (namely, the actual similarity of the individuals in amount of force and degree of worth, and their co-relation within one organisation). As soon, however, as one wished to take this principle more generally, and if possible even as *the fundamental principle of society,* it would immediately disclose what it really is—namely, a Will to the *denial* of life, a principle of dissolution and decay. Here one must think profoundly to the very basis and resist all sentimental weakness: life itself is *essentially* appropriation, injury, conquest of the strange and weak, suppression, severity, obtrusion of peculiar forms, incorporation, and at the least, putting it mildest, exploitation;—but why should one for ever use precisely these words on which for ages a disparaging purpose has been stamped? Even the organisation within which, as was previously supposed, the individuals treat each other as equal—it takes place in every healthy aristocracy—must itself, if it be a living and not a dying organisation, do all that towards other bodies, which the individuals within it refrain from doing to each other: it will have to be the incarnated Will to Power, it will endeavour to grow, to gain ground, attract to itself and acquire ascendency—not owing to any morality or immorality, but because it *lives,* and because life *is* precisely Will to Power. On no point, however, is the ordinary consciousness of Europeans more unwilling to be corrected than on this matter; people now rave everywhere, even under the guise of science, about coming conditions of society in which "the exploiting character" is to be absent:—that sounds to my ears as if they promised to invent a mode of life which should refrain from all organic functions. "Exploitation" does not belong to a depraved, or imperfect and primitive society: it belongs to the *nature* of the living being as a primary organic function; it is a consequence of the intrinsic Will to Power, which is precisely the Will to Life.—Granting that as a theory this is a novelty—as a reality it is the *fundamental fact* of all history: let us be so far honest towards ourselves!

In a tour through the many finer and coarser moralities which have hitherto prevailed or still prevail on the earth, I found certain traits recurring regularly together, and connected with one another, until finally two primary types revealed themselves to me, and a radical distinction was brought to light. There is *master-morality* and *slave-morality;*— I would at once add, however, that in all higher and mixed civilisations, there are also attempts at the reconciliation of the two moralities; but one finds still oftener the confusion and mutual misunderstanding of them, indeed, sometimes their close juxtaposition—even in the same man, within one soul. The distinctions of moral values have either originated in a ruling caste, pleasantly conscious of being different from the ruled—or among the ruled class, the slaves and dependents of all sorts. In the first case, when it is the rulers who determine the conception "good," it is the exalted, proud disposition which is regarded as the distinguishing feature, and that which determines the order of rank. The noble type of man separates from himself the beings in whom the opposite of this exalted, proud disposition displays itself: he despises them. Let it at once be noted that in this first kind of morality the antithesis "good" and "bad" means practically the same as "noble" and "despicable";—the antithesis "good" and *"evil"* is of different origin. The cowardly, the timid, the insignificant, and those thinking merely of narrow utility are despised; moreover, also, the distrustful, with their constrained glances, the self-abasing, the dog-like kind of men who let themselves be abused, the mendicant flatterers, and above all the liars:—it is a fundamental belief of all aristocrats that the common people are untruthful. "We truthful ones"—the nobility in ancient Greece called themselves. It is obvious that everywhere the designations of moral value were at first applied to *men,* and were only derivatively and at a later period applied to *actions;* it is a gross mistake, therefore, when historians of morals start with questions like, "Why have sympathetic actions been praised?" The noble type of man regards *himself* as a determiner of values; he does not require to be approved of; he passes the judgment: "What is injurious to me is injurious in itself"; he knows that it is he himself only who confers honour on things; he is a *creator of values.* He honours whatever he recognises in himself: such morality is self-glorification. In the foreground there is the feeling of plenitude, of power, which seeks to overflow, the happiness of high tension, the consciousness of a wealth which would fain give and bestow:—the noble man also helps the unfortunate, but not—or scarcely—out of pity, but rather from an impulse generated by the super-abundance of power. The noble man honours in himself the powerful one, him also who has power over himself, who knows how to speak and how to keep silence, who takes pleasure in subjecting himself to severity and hardness, and has reverence for all that is severe and hard. "Wotan placed a hard heart in my breast," says an old Scandinavian Saga: it is thus rightly expressed from the soul of a proud Viking. Such a type of man is even proud of *not* being made for sympathy; the hero of the Saga therefore adds warningly: "He who has not a hard heart when young, will never have one." The noble and brave who think thus are the furthest removed from the morality which sees precisely in sympathy, or in acting for the good of others, or in *désintéressement,* the characteristic of the moral; faith in oneself, pride in oneself, a radical enmity and irony towards "selflessness," belong as definitely to noble morality, as do a careless scorn and precaution in presence of sympathy and the "warm heart."—It is the powerful who *know* how to honour, it is their art, their domain for invention. The profound reverence for age and for tradition—all law rests on this double reverence,—the belief and prejudice in favour of ancestors and unfavourable to newcomers, is typical in the morality of the powerful; and if, reversely, men of "modern ideas" believe almost instinctively in "progress" and the "future," and are more and more lacking in respect for old age, the ignoble origin of these "ideas" has complacently betrayed itself thereby. A morality of the ruling class, however, is more especially foreign and irritating to present-day taste in the sternness of its principle that one has duties only to one's equals; that one may act towards beings of a lower rank, towards all that is foreign, just as seems good to one, or "as the heart desires," and in any case "beyond good and evil": it is here that sympathy and similar sentiments can have a place. The ability and obligation to exercise prolonged gratitude and prolonged revenge—both only within the circle of equals,—artfulness in retaliation, *raffinement* of the idea in friendship, a certain necessity to have enemies (as outlets for the emotions of envy, quarrelsomeness, arrogance—in fact, in order to be a good *friend*): all these are typical characteristics of the noble morality, which, as has been pointed out, is not the morality of "modern ideas," and is therefore at present difficult to realise and also to unearth and disclose.—It is otherwise with the second type of morality, *slave-morality*. Supposing that the abused, the oppressed, the suffering, the unemancipated, the weary, and those uncertain of themselves, should moralise, what will be the common element in their moral estimates? Probably a pessimistic suspicion with regard to the entire situation of man will find expression, perhaps a condemnation of man, together with his situation. The slave has an unfavourable eye for the virtues of the powerful; he has a scepticism and distrust, a *refinement* of distrust of everything "good" that is there honoured—he would fain persuade himself that the very happiness there is not genuine. On the other hand, *those* qualities which serve to alleviate the existence of sufferers are brought into prominence and flooded with light; it is here that sympathy, the kind, helping hand, the warm heart, patience, diligence, humility, and friendliness attain to honour; for here these are the most useful qualities, and almost the only means of supporting the burden of existence. Slave-morality is essentially the morality of utility.

Here is the seat of the origin of the famous antithesis "good" and "evil":—power and dangerousness are assumed to reside in the evil, a certain dreadfulness, subtlety, and strength, which do not admit of being despised. According to slave-morality, therefore, the "evil" man arouses fear; according to master-morality, it is precisely the "good" man who arouses fear and seeks to arouse it, while the bad man is regarded as the despicable being. The contrast attains its maximum when, in accordance with the logical consequences of slave-morality, a shade of depreciation—it may be slight and well-intentioned—at last attaches itself to the "good" man of this morality; because, according to the servile mode of thought, the good man must in any case be the *safe* man: he is good-natured, easily deceived, perhaps a little stupid, *un bonhomme*. Everywhere that slave-morality gains the ascendency, language shows a tendency to approximate the significations of the words "good" and "stupid."—A last fundamental difference: the desire for *freedom,* the instinct for happiness and the refinements of the feeling of liberty belong as necessarily to slave-morals and morality, as artifice and enthusiasm in reverence and devotion are the regular symptoms of an aristocratic mode of thinking and estimating. –Hence we can understand without further detail why love *as a passion*—it is our European specialty—must absolutely be of noble origin; as is well known, its invention is due to the Provencal poet-cavaliers, those brilliant, ingenious men of the *"gai saber,"* to whom Europe owes so much, and almost owes itself.

WILLIAM JAMES

(1842-1910)

"Not a victory is gained, not a deed of faithfulness or courage is done except upon a maybe; not a service, not a sally of generosity, not a scientific exploration or experiment or text-book, that may not be a mistake. It is only by risking our persons from one hour to another that we live at all."

William James was one of the earliest citizens of the United States to gain high regard in philosophical circles. Long associated with Harvard University where he taught physiology, psychology, and philosophy, James, in his major themes reflects a characteristically American attitude toward commitment, determination, and belief in action. Along with Charles Peirce, James developed the philosophy of Pragmatism, which emphasizes the practical importance of belief.

Two of James's most influential books reflect his interest in religion (*The Varieties of Religious Experience*) and psychology (*The Principles of Psychology*). James combined these two interests in a series of lectures at Harvard late in his life. Although he later observed that he should have called his talks "The Right to Believe," the original title has remained. A part of the concluding lecture in that series is presented here.

THE WILL TO BELIEVE

WILLIAM JAMES

And now, in turning to what religion may have to say to the question, I come to what is the soul of my discourse. Religion has meant many things in human history; but when from now onward I use the word I mean to use it in the supernaturalist sense, as declaring that the so-called order of nature, which constitutes this world's experience, is only one portion of the total universe, and that there stretches beyond this visible world an unseen world of which we now know nothing positive, but in its relation to which the true significance of our present mundane life consists. A man's religious faith (whatever more special items of doctrine it may involve) means for me essentially his faith in the existence of an unseen order of some kind in which the riddles of the natural order may be found explained. In the more developed religions the natural world has always been regarded as the mere scaffolding or vestibule of a truer, more eternal world, and affirmed to be a sphere of education, trial, or redemption. In these religions, one must in some fashion die to the natural life before one can enter into life eternal. The notion that this physical world of wind and water, where the sun rises and the moon sets, is absolutely and ultimately the divinely aimed-at and established thing, is one which we find only in very early religions, such as that of the most primitive Jews. It is this natural religion (primitive still, in spite of the fact that poets and men of science whose goodwill exceeds their perspicacity keep publishing it in new editions tuned to our contemporary ears) that, as I said a while ago, has suffered definitive bankruptcy in the opinion of a circle of persons, among whom I must count myself, and who are growing more numerous every day. For such persons the physical order of nature, taken simply as science knows it, cannot be held to reveal any one harmonious spiritual intent. It is mere *weather,* as Chauncey Wright called it, doing and undoing without end.

Now, I wish to make you feel, if I can in the short remainder of this hour, that we have a right to believe the physical order to be only a partial order; that we have a right to supplement it by an unseen spiritual order which we assume on trust, if only thereby life may seem to us better worth living again. But as such a trust will seem to some of you sadly mystical and execrably unscientific, I must first say a word or two to weaken the veto which you may consider that science opposes to our act.

There is included in human nature an ingrained naturalism and materialism of mind which can only admit facts that are actually tangible. Of this sort of mind the entity called "science" is the idol. Fondness for the word "scientist" is one of the notes by which you may know its votaries; and its short way of killing any opinion that it disbelieves in is to call it "unscientific." It must be granted that there is no slight excuse for this. Science has made such glorious leaps in the last three hundred years, and extended our knowledge of nature so enormously both in general and in detail; men of science, moreover, have as a class displayed such admirable virtues,—that it is no wonder if the worshippers of science lose their head. In this very University, accordingly, I have heard more than one teacher say that all the fundamental conceptions of truth have already been found by science, and that the future has only the details of the picture to fill in. But the slightest reflection on the real conditions will suffice to show how barbaric such notions are. They show such a lack of scientific imagination, that it is hard to see how one who is actively advancing any part of science can make a mistake so crude. Think how many absolutely new scientific conceptions have arisen in our own generation, how many new problems have been formulated that were never thought of before, and then cast an eye upon the brevity of science's career. It began with Galileo, not three hundred years ago. Four thinkers since Galileo, each informing his successor of what discoveries his own lifetime had seen achieved, might have passed the torch of science into our hands as we sit here in this room. Indeed, for the matter of that, an audience much smaller than the present one, an audience of some five or six score people, if each person in it could speak for his own generation, would carry us away to the black unknown of the human species, to days without a document or monument to tell their tale. Is it credible that such a mushroom knowledge, such a growth overnight as this, can represent more than the minutest glimpse of what the universe will really prove to be when adequately understood? No! Our science is a drop, our ignorance a sea. Whatever else be certain, this at least is certain,—that the world of our present natural knowledge is enveloped in a larger world of *some* sort of whose residual properties we at present can frame no positive idea.

Agnostic positivism, of course, admits this principle theoretically in the most cordial terms, but insists that we must not turn it to any practical use. We have no right, this doctrine tells us, to dream dreams, or suppose anything about the unseen part of the universe, merely because to do so may be for what we are pleased to call our highest interests. We must always wait for sensible evidence for our beliefs; and where such evidence is inaccessible we must frame no hypotheses whatever. Of course this is a safe enough position *in abstracto*. If a thinker had no stake in the unknown, no vital needs, to live or languish according to what the unseen world contained, a philosophic neutrality and refusal to believe either one way or the other would be his wisest cue. But, unfortunately, neutrality is not only inwardly difficult, it is also outwardly unrealizable, where our relations to an alternative are practical and vital. This is because, as the psychologists tell us, belief and doubt are living attitudes, and involve conduct on our part. Our only way, for example, of doubting or refusing to believe, that a certain thing *is,* is continuing to act as if it were *not.* If, for instance, I refuse to believe that the room is getting cold, I leave the windows open and light no fire just as if it still were warm. If I doubt that you are worthy of my confidence, I keep you uninformed of all my secrets just as if you were *un*worthy of the same. If I doubt the need of insuring my house, I leave it uninsured as much as if I believed there were no need. And so if I must not believe that the world is divine, I can only express that refusal by declining ever to act distinctively as if it were so, which can only mean acting on certain critical occasions as if it were *not* so, or in an irreligious way. There are, you see, inevitable occasions in life when inaction is a kind of action, and must count as action, and when not to be for is to be practically against; and in all such cases strict and consistent neutrality is an unattainable thing.

And, after all, is not this duty of neutrality, where only our inner interests would lead us to believe, the most ridiculous of commands? Is it not sheer dogmatic folly to say that our inner interests can have no real connection with the forces that the hidden world may contain? In other cases divinations based on inner interests have proved prophetic enough. Take science itself! Without an imperious inner demand on our part for ideal logical and mathematical harmonies, we should never have attained to proving that such harmonies lie hidden between all the chinks and interstices of the crude natural world. Hardly a law has been established in science, hardly a fact ascertained, which was not first sought after, often with sweat and blood, to gratify an inner need. Whence such needs come from we do not know: we find them in us, and biological psychology so far only classes them with Darwin's "accidental variations." But the inner need of believing that this world of nature is a sign of something more spiritual and eternal than itself is just as strong and authoritative in those who feel it, as the inner need of uniform laws of causation ever can be in a professionally scientific head. The toil of many generations has proved the latter need prophetic. Why *may* not the former one be prophetic, too? And if needs of ours outrun the visible universe, why *may* not that be sign that an invisible universe is there? What, in short, has authority to debar us from trusting our religious demands? Science as such assuredly has no authority, for she can only say what is, not what is not; and the agnostic "thou shalt not believe without coercive sensible evidence" is simply an expression (free to any one to make) of private personal appetite for evidence of a certain peculiar kind.

Now, when I speak of trusting our religious demands, just what do I mean by "trusting"? Is the word to carry with it license to define in detail an invisible world, and to anathematize and excommunicate those whose trust is different? Certainly not! Our faculties of belief were not primarily given us to make orthodoxies and heresies withal; they were given us to live by. And to trust our religious demands means first of all to live in the light of them, and to act as if the invisible world which they suggest were real. It is a fact of human nature, that men can live and die by the help of a sort of faith that goes without a single dogma of definition. The bare assurance that this natural order is not ultimate but a mere sign or vision, the eternal staging of a many-storied universe, in which spiritual forces have the last word and are eternal,—this bare assurance is to such men enough to make life seem worth living in spite of every contrary presumption suggested by its circumstances on the natural plane. Destroy this inner assurance, however, vague as it is, and all the light and radiance of existence is extinguished for these persons at a stroke. Often enough the wild-eyed look at life—the suicidal mood—will then set in.

And now the application comes directly home to you and me. Probably to almost everyone of us here the most adverse life would seem well worth living, if we only could be *certain* that our bravery and patience with it were terminating and eventuating and bearing fruit somewhere in an unseen spiritual world. By granting we are not certain, does it then follow that a bare trust in such a world is a fool's paradise and lubberland, or rather that it is a living attitude in which we are free to indulge? Well, we are free to trust at our own risks anything that is not impossible, and that can bring analogies to bear in its behalf. That the world of physics is probably not absolute, all the converging multitude of arguments that make in favor of idealism tend to prove; and that our whole physical life may lie soaking in a spiritual atmosphere, a dimension of being that we at present have no organ for apprehending, is vividly suggested to us by the analogy of our domestic animals. Our dogs, for example, are in our human life but not of it. They witness hourly the outward body of events whose inner meaning cannot, by any possible operation, be revealed to their intelligence,—events in which they themselves often play the cardinal part. My terrier bites a teasing boy, and the father demands damages. The dog may be present at every step of the negotiations, and see the money paid, without an inkling of what it all means, without a suspicion that it has anything to do with *him;* and he never *can* know in his natural dog's life. Or take another case which used greatly to impress me in my medical-student days. Consider a poor dog whom they are vivisecting in a laboratory. He lies strapped on a board and shrieking at his executioners, and to his own dark consciousness is literally in a sort of hell. He cannot see a single redeeming ray in the whole business; and yet all these diabolical—seeming events are often controlled by human intentions with which, if his poor benighted mind could only be made to catch a glimpse of them, all that is heroic in him would religiously acquiesce. Healing truth, relief to future sufferings of beast and man, are to be bought by them. It may be genuinely a process of redemption. Lying on his back on the board there he may be performing a function incalculably higher than any that prosperous canine life admits of; and yet, of the whole performance, this function is the one portion that must remain absolutely beyond his ken.

Now turn from this to the life of man. In the dog's life we see the world invisible to him because we live in both worlds. In human life, although we only see our world, and his within it, yet encompassing both these worlds a still wider world may be there, as unseen by us as our world is by him; and to believe in that world *may* be the most essential function that our lives in this world have to perform. But "*may* be! *may* be!" one now hears the positivist contemptuously exclaim; "what use can a scientific life have for maybes?" Well, I reply, the "scientific" life itself has much to do with maybes, and human life at large has everything to do with them. So far as man stands for anything, and is productive or originative at all, his entire vital function may be said to have to deal with maybes. Not a victory is gained, not a deed of faithfulness or courage is done, except upon a maybe; not a service, not a sally of generosity, not a scientific exploration or experiment or textbook, that may not be a mistake. It is only by risking our persons from one hour to another that we live at all. And often enough our faith beforehand in an uncertified result *is the only thing that makes the result come true.* Suppose, for instance, that you are climbing a mountain, and have worked yourself into a position from which the only escape is by a terrible leap. Have faith that you can successfully make it, and your feet are nerved to its accomplishment. But mistrust yourself, and think of all the sweet things you have heard the scientists say of *maybes,* and you will hesitate so long that, at last, all unstrung and trembling, and launching yourself in a moment of despair, you roll in the abyss. In such a case (and it belongs to an enormous class), the part of wisdom as well as of courage is to *believe what is in the line of your needs,* for only by such belief is the need fulfilled. Refuse to believe, and you shall indeed be right, for you shall irretrievably perish. But believe, and again you shall be right, for you shall save yourself. You make one or the other of two possible universes true by your trust or mistrust,—both universes having been only *maybes,* in this particular, before you contributed your act.

Now, it appears to me that the questions whether life is worth living is subject to conditions logically much like these. It does, indeed, depend on you *the liver.* If you surrender to the nightmare view and crown the evil edifice by your own suicide, you have indeed made a picture totally black. Pessimism, completed by your act, is true beyond a doubt, so far as your world goes. Your mistrust of life has removed whatever worth your own enduring existence might have given to it; and now, throughout the whole sphere of possible influence of that existence, the mistrust has proved itself to have had divining power. But suppose, on the other hand, that instead of giving way to the nightmare view, you cling to it that this world is not the *ultimatum.* Suppose you find yourself a very wellspring, as Wordsworth says, of—

> Zeal and the virtue to exist by faith
> As soldiers live by courage; as, by strength
> Of heart, the sailor fights with roaring seas.

Suppose, however thickly evils crowd upon you, that your unconquerable subjectivity proves to be their match, and that you find a more wonderful joy than any passive pleasure can bring in trusting ever in the large whole. Have you not now made life worth living on these terms? What sort of a thing would life really be, with your qualities ready for a tussle with it, if it only brought fair weather and gave these higher faculties of yours no scope? Please remember that optimism and pessimism are definitions of the world, and that our own reactions on the world, small as they are in bulk, are integral parts of the whole thing, and necessarily help to determine the definition. They may even be the decisive elements in determining the definition. A large mass can have its unstable equilibrium overturned by the addition of a feather's weight; a long phrase may have its sense reversed by the addition of the three letters n-o-t. This life *is* worth living, we can say, *since it is what we make it, from the moral point of view;* and we are determined to make it from that point of view, so far as we have anything to do with it, a success.

Now, in this description of faiths that verify themselves I have assumed that our faith in an invisible order is what inspires those efforts and that patience which make this visible order good for moral men. Our faith in the seen world's goodness (goodness now meaning fitness for successful moral and religious life) has verified itself by leaning on our faith in the unseen world. But will our faith in the unseen world similarly verify itself? Who knows?

Once more is a case of *maybe;* and once more *maybes* are the essence of the situation. I confess that I do not see why the very existence of an invisible world may not in part depend on the personal response which any one of us may make to the religious appeal. God himself, in short, may draw vital strength and increase of very being from our fidelity. For my own part, I do not know what the sweat and blood and tragedy of this life mean, if they mean anything short of this. If this life be not a real fight, in which something is eternally gained for the universe by success, it is no better than a game of private theatricals from which one may withdraw at will. But it *feels* like a real fight,— as if there were something really wild in the universe which we, with all our idealities and faithfulnesses, are needed to redeem; and first of all to redeem our own hearts from atheisms and fears. For such a half-wild, half-saved universe our nature is adapted. The deepest thing in our nature is this *Binnenleben* (as a German doctor lately has called it), this dumb region of the heart in which we dwell alone with our willingnesses and unwillingnesses, our faiths and fears. As through the cracks and crannies of caverns those waters exude from the earth's bossom which then form the fountain-heads of springs, so in these crepuscular depths of personality the sources of all our outer deeds and decisions take their rise. Here is our deepest organ of communication with the nature of things; and compared with all these concrete movements of our soul all abstract statements and scientific arguments—the veto, for example, which the strict positivist pronounces upon our faith— sound to us like mere chatterings of the teeth. For here possibilities, not finished facts, are the realities with which we have acutely to deal; and to quote my friend William Salter, of the Philadelphia Ethical Society, "as the essence of courage is to stake one's life on a possibility, so the essence of faith is to believe that the possibility exists."

These, then, are my last words to you: Be *not* afraid of life. Believe that life *is* worth living, and your belief will help create the fact. The "scientific proof" that you are right may not be clear before the day of judgment (or some stage of being which that expression may serve to symbolize) is reached. But the faithful fighters of this hour, or the beings that then and there will represent them, may turn to the fainthearted, who here decline to go on, with words like those with which Henry IV greeted the tardy Crillon after a great victory had been gained: "Hang yourself, brave Crillon! we fought at Arques, and you were not there."

SOURCES

The readings in this anthology were selected from previously published sources.

The Apology of Socrates (Plato). From *Greek and Roman Classics in Translation*. Translated by Benjamin Jewett.

The Republic (Plato). From *Greek and Roman Classics in Translation*. Translated by Benjamin Jewett.

Nicomachean Ethics (Aristotle). From *Greek and Roman Classics in Translation*. Translated by W.D. Ross.

Letter to Menoecius (Epicurus). From *The Way of Philosophy*. Translated by Philip Wheelwright.

The Enchiridion (Epictetus). Translated by Thomas W. Higginson. Bobbs-Merrill Educational Publishing.

Meditations (Marcus Aurelius). From *Outline of Great Books*, J.A. Hammerton, editor.

Confessions (Augustine). From *Outline of Great Books*, J.A. Hammerton, editor.

Novum Organum (Bacon). From *The English Philosophers from Bacon to Mill*, Edwin A. Burtt, editor.

Leviathan (Hobbes). From *Outline of Great Books*, J.A. Hammerton, editor.

Discourse on Method (Descartes). From *Outline of Great Books*, J.A. Hammerton, editor.

On the Improvement of the Understanding (Spinoza). Translated by R.H.M. Elwes. Dover Publications, Inc.

Essay Concerning Human Understanding (Locke). From *Outline of Great Books*, J.A. Hammerton, editor.

The Social Contract (Rousseau). From *Outline of Great Books*, J.A. Hammerton, editor.

Essays Moral and Political (Hume). From *Outline of Great Books*, J.A. Hammerton, editor.

Fundamental Principles of the Metaphysic of Morals (Kant). Translated by Thomas K. Abbott. Bobbs-Merril Educational Publishing.

The Philosophy of Religion (Hegel). From *Outline of Great Books*, J.A. Hammerton, editor.

On the Basis of Morality (Schopenhauer). Translated by E.F.J. Payne. Bobbs-Merrill Educational Publishing.

Utilitarianism (Mill). Bobbs-Merrill Educational Publishing.

The Attack Upon "Christendom" (Kierkegaard). From *A Kierkegaard Anthology*. Translated by Walter Lowrie.

Beyond Good and Evil (Nietzsche). Translated by Helen Zimmern. Modern Library.

The Will to Believe (James). From *The Odyssey Reader,* Newman P. and Genevieve Birk, editors.

www.ingramcontent.com/pod-product-compliance
Lightning Source LLC
Chambersburg PA
CBHW060509090426
42735CB00011B/2151